Preparing for the Texas Algebra I End-of-Course Exam

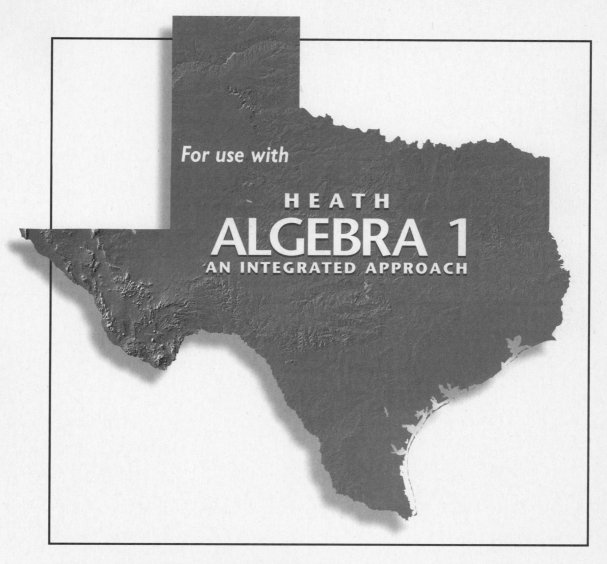

For use with

HEATH
ALGEBRA 1
AN INTEGRATED APPROACH

The Preparing for the Texas Algebra I End-of-Course Exam *booklet includes EOC practice exams, in-class activities, and practice worksheets to help students prepare for the EOC exam. Also included are a correlation of the EOC objectives to pages in the Student Edition textbook and in several ancillaries, a formula chart, answer sheets to be used with the EOC practice exams, and a summary sheet to track a student's progress.*

McDougal Littell
A HOUGHTON MIFFLIN COMPANY
Evanston, Illinois • Boston • Dallas

ISBN: 0-669-45516-4

456789 – HWI – 01 00 99

CONTENTS

Note to the Teacher:
Changes to the Algebra I EOC Exam

In the fall of 1996, the Algebra I End-of-Course (EOC) Exam was revised to make it more closely reflect the new Texas Essential Knowledge and Skills (TEKS). In particular, the number of questions used to assess each EOC objective has in some cases changed, although the total number of questions on the exam remains at 40.

The specific changes made to the EOC exam are as follows:

▸ Objectives 2 and 3, which require students to graph linear equations and inequalities and write equations of lines, are now *each* assessed with four questions. Previously, a combined total of six questions was used to assess *both* objectives.

▸ The first instructional target for Objective 5, which requires students to solve absolute value equations and inequalities, is no longer assessed on the EOC exam. However, the number of questions used to assess Objective 5 remains at four.

▸ Objective 7, which requires students to solve rational and radical equations, is no longer assessed on the EOC exam.

▸ Objective 9, which requires students to use problem-solving strategies to analyze, solve, and/or justify solutions to problems involving one-variable or two-variable situations, is now assessed with eight questions instead of six.

All of these changes have been incorporated into the two EOC practice exams on pages 37–56 of this booklet. However, because some teachers may still want to assess Objective 7 and the first instructional target of Objective 5 (even though these are no longer assessed on the EOC exam), a set of optional questions that cover these objectives has been included at the end of each EOC practice exam.

In addition, some of the classroom review activities and practice worksheets in this booklet have exercises relating to Objective 7 and the first instructional target of Objective 5. Each such exercise has been labeled "optional" to indicate that the topic it covers is no longer assessed on the EOC exam.

Note to the Student: Test-Taking Strategies

Algebra students in Texas are required to take the End-of-Course (EOC) Examination for Algebra I. This test is primarily in a multiple-choice format, with a limited number of open-ended questions. It consists of forty questions, and is based on nine of the following ten original objectives:

1 understanding the characteristics of graphing in problems

2 graphing lines, linear inequalities in one or two variables, and systems of inequalities

3 writing equations of lines to model problems

4 writing and solving linear equations, inequalities, and systems of linear equations

5 writing and solving quadratic equations

6 adding, subtracting, multiplying, dividing, and factoring polynomials

7 solving rational and radical equations (Note: This objective is no longer tested on the End-of-Course Examination.)

8 using problem-solving strategies to analyze, solve, and justify solutions to real-world and mathematical problems involving exponents, quadratic equations, and right triangles

9 using problem-solving strategies to analyze, solve, and justify solutions to real-world and mathematical problems involving one-variable equations and inequalities and systems of equations

10 using problem-solving strategies to analyze, solve, and justify solutions to real-world and mathematical problems involving probability, ratio and proportion, and data displayed in graphs and tables

By preparing for the test and using some simple test-taking strategies, you can approach the EOC exam with confidence.

Preparing for the EOC Exam

The best way to prepare for the EOC exam is to be an active learner throughout the school year.

KEEP UP with your class preparation, notes, and assignments.

REVIEW YOUR NOTES every day to be sure that you understand all the important vocabulary words and skills introduced in that day's lesson.

IF YOU USE A SCIENTIFIC OR GRAPHING CALCULATOR in your algebra class, be sure you learn how to operate the calculator. Although you are allowed to use a calculator on the EOC exam, you will not be permitted to bring a user's manual or any other materials with you to the exam. You also will not be permitted to have any programs.

DEVELOP TECHNIQUES, such as flash cards, that help you practice and remember the ideas and skills that you need to know.

TAKE A SAMPLE EXAM, if possible, to help you identify any weak areas you may have.

The Night Before the Exam

The night before the exam is a good time to relax and review your strategies for taking the exam.

AVOID LAST-MINUTE CRAMMING; trying to learn new material the night before the exam will not be helpful.

AVOID ARGUMENTS. Try to spend the evening in a good, relaxed mood. Stay in a positive frame of mind. Remember that the exam is an opportunity to show what you know.

SET OUT NECESSITIES, such as sharpened pencils, an eraser, your glasses if you wear them, and tissues so you won't forget them. You may want to bring a quick-energy snack in case you become hungry or tired while taking the exam.

GET A GOOD NIGHT'S SLEEP.

The Day of the Exam

Here are some tips to help you get ready to take the exam:

GET UP EARLY ENOUGH so that you won't need to hurry.

EAT A GOOD BREAKFAST, but avoid overeating or trying something new.

CHOOSE COMFORTABLE CLOTHES. (Save your new clothes or shoes for another day.) You might dress in layers so you can adjust your clothing if the testing room seems too warm or too cold.

BRING YOUR CALCULATOR if you have one and have been using it in algebra class. You might also bring spare batteries for the calculator in case you need them. (If you do not own a calculator, do not worry. Your school is required to make a calculator available to you during the exam.)

BE SURE TO ARRIVE AT SCHOOL ON TIME. Stay calm and in a positive frame of mind.

Taking the EOC Exam

To be successful with the EOC exam, take control of the situation. Decide that you will stay calm and choose strategies that will work for you.

Before the Exam Begins

Focus on yourself while you are in the testing room. Pay no attention to when others start or finish, or whether others appear anxious or not. Before the exam begins, take a few minutes to sit quietly. Take a few slow, deep breaths, and relax any muscles that are tight. Tell yourself that you will do your best and will not blame yourself for what you do not know.

Strategies for Taking the Exam

Think about the following list of strategies and decide which ones will help you. You will be allowed a minimum of two hours to take the exam. Find out if additional testing time will be allowed.

PACE YOURSELF, working carefully and smoothly. Do not rush through the exam since that may result in careless errors or feelings of panic. However, avoid spending too much time on one question.

WHEN YOU BEGIN TAKING THE EXAM, work quickly through the entire exam, answering only the questions you can do easily. As you go through the

exam, cross off answer choices that you know are incorrect, put a check mark next to questions you have answered and feel sure of, and circle or star each question number that you plan to come back to. If you skip a question in your exam booklet, be sure to skip the question on your answer sheet also. When you go back through the exam a second time, continue to use the same marking system. Each time you complete four to six questions, stop and check if your answer numbers match your question numbers.

READ EACH QUESTION and all the answer choices carefully. Be sure that you understand what the question asks and that you do not overlook a key word or phrase. Reread any question that you do not understand fully.

INCLUDED IN THE EXAM are some open-ended questions. Such questions may ask for a numerical answer or a graph. There may be a wide variety of correct answers for an open-ended question, or just one. When you are answering an open-ended question, be careful to follow the directions. A numerical answer grid contains a decimal point; be sure to position your answer correctly with respect to the decimal point. If you are asked to graph a line, the graph should extend to the edges of the grid. If you are asked to graph an inequality in two variables, you should shade the entire solution region shown.

IF YOU WERE TAUGHT in your algebra class to solve a particular type of problem using a calculator, then use a calculator when you encounter the same type of problem on the exam. You can also use the calculator to check work done by using paper and pencil. But do not assume that the calculator is always right: if you press the wrong keys, the calculator will give you incorrect results.

YOU MAY WRITE IN YOUR EXAM BOOKLET or use a highlighter to emphasize important parts of a problem if you find that helpful. As you read a question, circle or underline key information or words in it, such as *total, about,* and *least.* Also cross out any unnecessary information. Draw pictures or diagrams to help you visualize a problem. Put a mark next to questions that you may be able to answer but need more time to complete.

YOU DO NOT NEED TO MEMORIZE FORMULAS. Included in your exam booklet is a page with a formula chart. The chart lists formulas related to perimeter, circumference, area, surface area, and volume, along with the Pythagorean theorem, the distance formula,

the slope formula, the quadratic formula, the slope-intercept form of an equation, the point-slope form of an equation, and the standard form of an equation. Refer to the formulas on this page as needed. You may write on this page, for example, to underline a particular formula, if you wish.

EXAMINE YOUR ANSWER SHEET to see that it is marked correctly. When erasing, be careful that your marks are erased completely. Check frequently that the answer number matches the question number.

YOUR SCORE IS BASED on the number of questions you answer correctly. You should answer every question even if you have to guess. Read all the answer choices, crossing out the ones that are clearly incorrect. Look for numbers that are obviously too large or too small and for relationships that do not make sense. If two answers mean the same thing, both are incorrect. If two answers have opposite values, one is likely to be correct. Watch out for answers that are partially correct or only answer part of the question; an answer that is not completely true is an incorrect answer. Try to eliminate at least a few choices and then make your best guess from the remaining choices.

IF YOU DO NOT KNOW THE ANSWER to a question, scan the answer choices for ideas of how to approach the problem. You may be able to work backward from the answer choices. For example, you can test a number that is "in the middle." If your result is too large, try a smaller answer choice.

SOME QUESTIONS will require more than one step to answer. Work out all the steps carefully and completely. The answer to each preliminary step may be listed as an answer choice, but only one is the final, correct answer.

VERY FEW QUESTIONS on previous Algebra I EOC Exams have had the answer "Not Here." Therefore, check your work very carefully when choosing that answer for a question. Remember that there can be several correct forms for an answer; for example, you might think that the correct answer for a question is 0.25, when the correct answer choice is $\frac{1}{4}$ or 25%.

EXAMINE YOUR ANSWERS to see that they are reasonable. Estimation can be used to verify an answer choice or to eliminate one or more answer choices.

TO SOLVE A WORD PROBLEM, read the problem quickly to understand the main ideas, identify the unknown quantity, and look over the answer choices. Then go back and read the problem slowly and carefully. Remember that some problems contain unnecessary information. Select the information you need and do not be concerned if you do not use all the information that is given.

STAY FOCUSED ON THE EXAM. Try to avoid thinking about your emotional and physical feelings or about other topics unrelated to the exam. If your attention starts to wander or you begin to feel tense, refocus your attention on the exam or take a short break: breathe deeply, relax your body, and replace negative thoughts with positive, supportive thoughts. For example, if you start thinking "I feel so nervous, and my head hurts. Something must be wrong with me," replace that thought with this one: "I'll take some deep breaths and use relaxation techniques to control my nervousness. Then I'll be able to focus on the exam." Instead of getting upset if you cannot answer a question, simply circle the question to read again later and go on to a different question. You may be able to answer the question easily later in the exam period.

WHEN YOU ARE FINISHED answering all the questions, read the exam carefully from the beginning to the end to check your work, if you have enough time to do so. You should check that you have marked each answer in the correct place, that you have not left any answer blank or marked more than one answer for any question, and that your answer sheet contains no stray marks or incomplete erasures.

REMEMBER: This exam is just one of many that you have taken over the years. It covers skills that you have already learned. By selecting strategies that are appropriate for you, you can approach the EOC exam confident that you will do your best.

Correlation of *Heath Algebra 1: An Integrated Approach* to the End-of-Course (EOC) Objectives

EOC OBJECTIVES and Instructional Targets	Student Edition and Teacher's Edition	Extra Practice Copymasters	Reteaching Copymasters
OBJECTIVE 1 **Demonstrate an understanding of the characteristics of graphing in problems involving real-world and mathematical situations.**			
Describe the domains and ranges of various functions and relations	pp. 242–248, 458–464, 472–477, 479–485, 588–593, 620–625, 695–701	pp. 60, 62–63	pp. 60, 62–63
Identify the effects of simple parameter changes on the graphs of relations and linear, quadratic, and absolute value functions	pp. 197–210, 217–222, 236–248, 465–485	pp. 28, 30, 32–33, 61–63	pp. 28, 30, 32–33, 61–63
OBJECTIVE 2 **Graph problems involving real-world and mathematical situations.**			
Graph a line given its characteristics or equation	pp. 176–222	pp. 24–30	pp. 24–30
Graph linear inequalities in one or two variables	pp. 292–297, 305–311, 320–326	pp. 39, 41, 43	pp. 39, 41, 43
Graph systems of inequalities and recognize the solution(s) from the graph	pp. 381–392	pp. 50–51	pp. 50–51
OBJECTIVE 3 **Write equations of lines to model problems involving real-world and mathematical situations.**			
Write an equation of a line given its graph or description	pp. 235–289	pp. 32–38	pp. 32–38
OBJECTIVE 4 **Formulate or solve linear equations/inequalities and systems of linear equations that describe real-world and mathematical situations.**			
Formulate or solve linear equations/inequalities	pp. 141–146, 235–289, 292–326, 492–497, 568–580, 626–632	pp. 20, 32–43, 65, 74–75, 82	pp. 20, 32–43, 65, 74–75, 82
Formulate or solve systems of linear equations	pp. 345–397	pp. 45–51	pp. 45–51

Correlation of *Heath Algebra 1: An Integrated Approach* to the End-of-Course (EOC) Objectives

EOC OBJECTIVES and Instructional Targets	Student Edition and Teacher's Edition	Extra Practice Copymasters	Reteaching Copymasters
OBJECTIVE 5 Formulate or solve absolute value equations/inequalities and quadratic equations that describe real-world and mathematical situations.			
Solve absolute value equations/inequalities*	pp. 223–228, 313–319, 492–497	pp. 31, 42, 65	pp. 31, 42, 65
Formulate or solve quadratic equations	pp. 458–463, 472–485, 492–497, 541–554, 639–644	pp. 60, 62–63, 65, 71–72, 84	pp. 60, 62–63, 65, 71–72, 84
OBJECTIVE 6 Perform operations on and factor polynomials that describe real-world and mathematical situations.			
Perform operations on polynomials	pp. 508–527	pp. 66–68	pp. 66–68
Factor polynomials using models	pp. 528–533, 535–554	pp. 69–72	pp. 69–72
OBJECTIVE 7 Solve rational and radical equations that describe real-world and mathematical situations.*			
Solve rational equations	pp. 562–567, 607–612, 646–650	pp. 73, 80, 85	pp. 73, 80, 85
Solve radical equations	pp. 695–700	p. 91	p. 91
OBJECTIVE 8 Use problem-solving strategies to analyze, solve, and/or justify solutions to real-world and mathematical problems involving exponents, quadratic situations, or right triangles.			
Analyze and/or solve problems involving the laws of exponents	pp. 399–449, 492–497, 633–638	pp. 52–58, 65, 83	pp. 52–58, 65, 83
Analyze and/or solve problems involving quadratic situations	pp. 458–503, 541–554, 639–644	pp. 60–65, 71–72, 84	pp. 60–65, 71–72, 84
Analyze and/or solve problems involving right triangles	pp. 452–457, 676–681, 703–709	pp. 59, 88, 92	pp. 59, 88, 92

*This instructional target or objective will no longer be assessed.

Correlation of *Heath Algebra 1: An Integrated Approach* to the End-of-Course (EOC) Objectives

EOC OBJECTIVES and Instructional Targets	Student Edition and Teacher's Edition	Extra Practice Copymasters	Reteaching Copymasters
OBJECTIVE 9 Use problem-solving strategies to analyze, solve, and/or justify solutions to real-world and mathematical problems involving one-variable or two-variable situations.			
Analyze and/or solve problems involving one-variable situations	pp. 39–46, 122–159, 292–319, 458–464, 472–485, 541–554, 562–574, 607–612, 626–651, 695–701	pp. 7, 17–22, 39–42, 60, 62–63, 71–74, 80, 82–85, 91	pp. 7, 17–22, 39–42, 60, 62–63, 71–74, 80, 82–85, 91
Analyze and/or solve problems involving two-variable situations	pp. 183–289, 320–326, 345–397, 432–444, 575–580	pp. 25–38, 43, 45–51, 57–58, 75	pp. 25–38, 43, 45–51, 57–58, 75
OBJECTIVE 10 Use problem-solving strategies to analyze, solve, and/or justify solutions to real-world and mathematical problems involving probability, ratio and proportion, or graphical and tabular data.			
Analyze and/or solve problems involving probability	pp. 581–586	p. 76	p. 76
Analyze and/or solve problems involving ratio and proportion	pp. 107–113, 562–580, 607–612	pp. 16, 73–75, 80	pp. 16, 73–75, 80
Analyze graphical and tabular data including scatter plots and/or make predictions based on this data	pp. 49–54, 160–166, 255–262, 327–333, 492–497, 652–664	pp. 8, 23, 35, 44, 65, 86–87	pp. 8, 23, 35, 44, 65, 86–87

Domain-and-Range

Activity for Objective 1

Number of players: 2

Materials:
- Domain-and-Range Game Board
- Answer Key
- calculator
- sheets of paper
- pencil

Directions:

Place the game board between the players, using a blank sheet of paper to cover the problems. When the players are ready, slide the blank sheet of paper down to reveal the first problem. Each player calculates the corresponding range value for each of the four domain values given. After both players have finished, they check each other's results. If the answers do not match, the players try to determine which response is correct. If they are unable to determine this, they may check the Answer Key for the correct response. Follow the same procedure for all 10 rounds. The winner is the player with the most points at the end of the game.

Scoring:

The players score points for each correct response, with four points possible in each round. If the player who finishes first gets all four responses correct, then that player gets two extra bonus points. The player with the most points at the end of the 10 rounds is declared the winner.

Domain-and-Range, *continued*

Game Board for "Domain-and-Range"

Activity for Objective 1

Function	Find the range for the given domain. X column
1. $f(x) = x^2 + 2$ $y = (-7)^2 + 2$ $y = x^2 + 2$ $y = 51$	**1.** $D = \{-7, -1, 4, 12\}$
2. $f(x) = 3x + 2$ $y = 3x + 2$	**2.** $D = \{-10, -5, 5, 10\}$
3. $f(x) = 2x - 5$	**3.** $D = \{0, \frac{1}{2}, \frac{3}{4}, 3\}$
4. $f(x) = 4x^2 + x - 7$	**4.** $D = \{2, 4, 6, 8\}$
5. $f(x) = 0.5(x - 1) + 2$	**5.** $D = \{-3, -1, 1, 3\}$
6. $f(x) = x^2 - 11$	**6.** $D = \{-6, -3, 2, 11\}$
7. $f(x) - 3 = 5(x - 4)$	**7.** $D = \{12, 15, 19, 25\}$
8. $f(x) = \frac{x-1}{3}$	**8.** $D = \{-5, 4, 13, 22\}$
9. $f(x) = 2x^2 - 4x$	**9.** $D = \{0, \frac{1}{4}, \frac{1}{2}, 1\}$
10. $f(x) = -4x^2 - 5x + 10$ press 2nd graph $y =$	**10.** $D = \{-4, 0, 6, 9\}$

Preparing for the Texas Algebra I End-of-Course Exam
Copyright © McDougal Littell Inc. All rights reserved.

Graph Match

Activity for Objective 2

Number of players: 2–3
Materials:
- one set of Graph Match Cards
- Answer Key
- graph paper
- pencil

Directions:

The 48 game cards consist of 24 matching pairs; each pair consists of a linear inequality and its graph. The two decks are first shuffled separately by one of the players, who then deals six cards to each of the three players, three from each deck. (If there are two players, then each player receives four cards from each deck.) The remaining cards are then placed face down on the playing surface and the top card turned face up alongside the deck. The players examine their cards and, without revealing their hand, start to match up any inequality cards and graph cards that they may have. The objective of the game is to get rid of all six (or all eight) cards in one's hand by matching inequality cards and graph cards. As an aid in identifying matching cards, players may sketch graphs on the graph paper provided. At any time, if a player has a match, then he or she places those two cards face up.

The player at the left of the dealer goes first. Player 1 first lays down any matching pairs she has in her hand. She then draws either the card that has been turned over or the top card from the remaining deck. If it matches a card in her hand, she places the matched set down in front of her and discards a card from her hand. If the card she drew is not a matching card, she may either discard it or place it in her hand and discard another card. Play continues to the left, with the next player proceeding in the same manner. The winner is the first player to lay down all of his or her cards.

If a player makes a mistake in matching an inequality card and a graph card and is challenged by one of the other players, then he has to retrieve not only those two cards but also an additional pair of cards from the deck. If there is a disagreement about a particular match, the players can consult the Answer Key. If all the cards in the deck have been used and there is no winner, then the discard pile is shuffled and reused. The game continues, with the top card turned face up alongside the deck of face-down cards.

Note: Each group of players should have one copy of pages 4–6 to cut out the graph cards and inequality cards.

Graph Match, *continued*

Cards for "Graph Match": Graphs

Activity for Objective 2

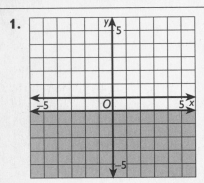

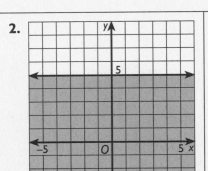

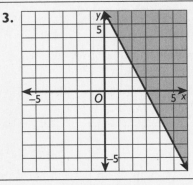

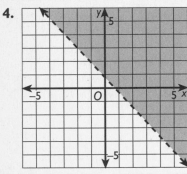

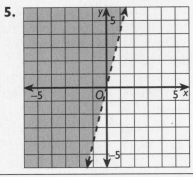

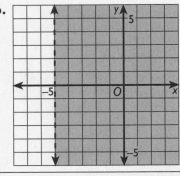

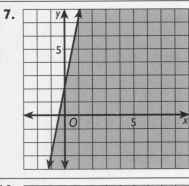

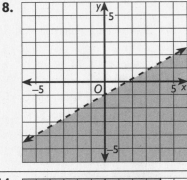

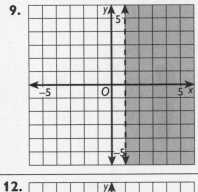

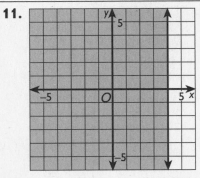

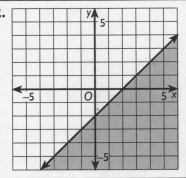

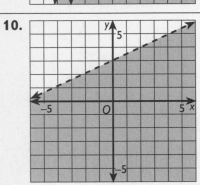

Preparing for the Texas Algebra I End-of-Course Exam

Graph Match, *continued*

Cards for "Graph Match": Graphs

Activity for Objective 2

13.
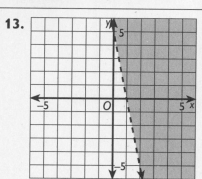

14.
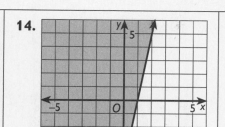

15.
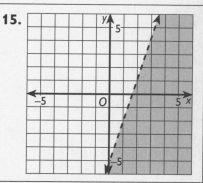

16.
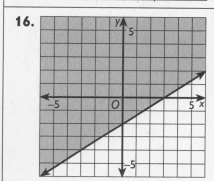

17.
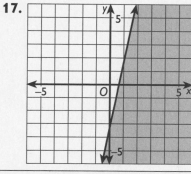

18.
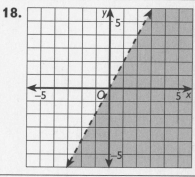

19.
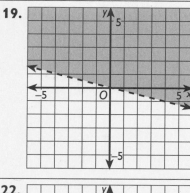

20.
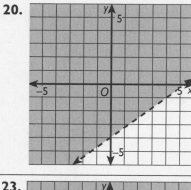

21.
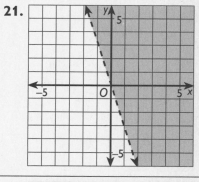

22.
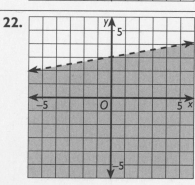

23.
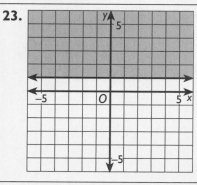

24.
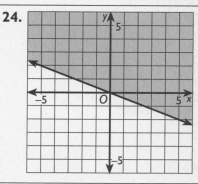

Graph Match, *continued*

Cards for "Graph Match": Inequalities

Activity for Objective 2

1. $y < 2x$	**2.** $y \leq 5x + 2$	**3.** $y > -3x$
4. $x \leq 4$	**5.** $y < \frac{1}{5}x + 3$	**6.** $y \leq 5$
7. $y > -5x + 5$	**8.** $y \geq 5x - 5$	**9.** $x > 1$
10. $y \geq -2x + 6$	**11.** $y < 3x - 5$	**12.** $y \leq -1$
13. $y > \frac{3}{4}x - 4$	**14.** $y \leq x - 2$	**15.** $x > -5$
16. $y \leq 5x - 3$	**17.** $y < \frac{3}{5}x - 1$	**18.** $y \geq 1$
19. $y < \frac{1}{2}x + 3$	**20.** $y \geq -\frac{2}{5}x$	**21.** $y > 4x$
22. $y \geq \frac{2}{3}x - 2$	**23.** $y > -x + 1$	**24.** $y > -\frac{1}{4}x$

Roll Out That Equation!

Activity for Objective 3

Number of players: 3

Materials:
- three Point Cards
- standard pair of dice
- Answer Key for each Point Card
- calculator
- sheets of paper
- pencil

Directions:

The game is played in three rounds; in each round, two players play and the third player acts as referee. In Round One, the referee is given the Answer Key for that round, and each of the players is given a die. Each of the three Point Cards shows an ordered number pair that represents the coordinates of a point in the coordinate plane.

The Point Card for Round One is placed between the two players. They each roll the die in order to determine the coordinates of a second point. When the dice are rolled, the greater number is used as the *x*-coordinate and the lesser number is the *y*-coordinate. If the numbers rolled are the same, then those numbers are used for both coordinates. Once the coordinates of the second point have been determined, the two players race to write the slope-intercept form of the equation of the line that contains both points. Any fraction must be expressed in simplest form. The first player to get the correct answer is awarded two points.

If the first player to finish submits an incorrect answer to the referee, then one point is subtracted from his or her score and the second player has the opportunity to earn the two points by finding the correct equation. If the second player's answer is also incorrect, then he or she also loses one point. Players then continue the game by rolling the dice again. The first player to accumulate 15 or more points is the winner of that round. For all three rounds, the players rotate between being the referee and playing the game.

Note: Each group of players should have one copy of page 8 to cut out the Point Cards.

Roll Out That Equation!, *continued*

Point Cards for "Roll Out That Equation!"

Activity for Objective 3

Round 1

$$(-3, -2), (\underline{\hspace{1.5em}}, \underline{\hspace{1.5em}})$$

Round 2

$$(-6, -1), (\underline{\hspace{1.5em}}, \underline{\hspace{1.5em}})$$

Round 3

$$(-1, -4), (\underline{\hspace{1.5em}}, \underline{\hspace{1.5em}})$$

8

Slope of a Line

Activity for Objective 4

Directions:

Find the slopes of the 10 lines defined by the equations in the left column. For each equation, start at the point that is immediately to its right, on the left side of the grid. From that point, draw a line that has the same slope as the line defined by the equation. (The first line is drawn for you.) The line will pass through a point labeled with a letter of the alphabet. Write that letter in the square at the bottom of the page that corresponds to the problem number. Then answer the following riddle:

Who is a mathematics teacher's favorite comedian/movie star?

1. $y + 3x = 5$

2. $2y + x = -8$

3. $-1(y + 3) = x + 3$

4. $y - x = 3$

5. $4y = x - 12$

6. $3y - 2x = 15$

7. $20 = 8y - 16x$

8. $7(y - 3) = -x - 21$

9. $\frac{3}{10}y - \frac{1}{2}x = \frac{9}{5}$

10. $\frac{1}{4}y - \frac{1}{5}x = \frac{1}{2}$

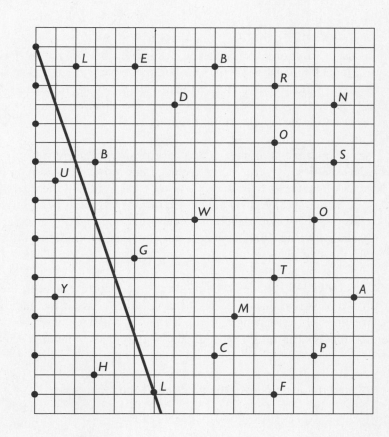

Problem Number:	3	6	9	2	7	10	1	5	8	4
Letter:							L			

The Quadratic Race

Activity for Objective 5

> **Number of players:** 2–4
> **Materials:**
> - Quadratic Race Cards
> - Quadratic Race Game Board
> - game piece for each player
> - Answer Key
> - calculator
> - paper
> - pencil

Directions:

Place the game board in front of the players and position each of their game pieces on one of the black circles. Place the shuffled game cards, face down, next to the game board. When the players are ready, turn the first game card over to reveal a quadratic equation. Each player then solves the equation using any method, including factoring or the Quadratic Formula.

Every equation has been selected to have at least one positive answer. If both answers are positive, the first player to solve the equation moves his game piece forward by the greater positive answer. If one answer is positive and the other answer negative, the winning player has the choice of moving his or her game piece forward by the positive value, or moving one of the opponents' pieces backward by the negative value. If an answer is not an integer, round it to the nearest integer, and use that value.

If, after a player has moved, he or she is found to have an incorrect answer, then the player must move back five lines (or back to the starting circle if the game piece is within five lines of the starting circles). If there is a disagreement about an answer, then the players can refer to the Answer Key to determine the correct answer.

The first player to land on or cross over the goal line is the winner.

Note: Each group of players should have one copy of pages 11–13 to cut out the game board and game cards.

Game Board for "The Quadratic Race"

Activity for Objective 5

1. _____
2. _____
3. _____
4. _____
5. _____
6. _____
7. _____
8. _____
9. _____
10. _____
11. _____
12. _____
13. _____
14. _____
15. _____
16. _____
17. _____
18. _____
19. _____
20. _____
21. _____
22. _____
23. _____
24. _____
25. _____

_____ G ____ O ____ A ____ L _____ L ____ I ____ N ____ E _____

The Quadratic Race, *continued*

Cards for "The Quadratic Race"

Activity for Objective 5

1. $x^2 + 2x - 15 = 0$	**2.** $x^2 - 7x + 6 = 0$
3. $x^2 - 12x = -20$	**4.** $x^2 - 4x - 12 = 0$
5. $4x^2 = 11x - 6$	**6.** $5x^2 - 35x + 60 = 0$
7. $x^2 - 8x + 15 = 0$	**8.** $x^2 + 18 = 9x$
9. $x^2 - 9x + 11 = 0$	**10.** $2x^2 - 5x + 2 = 0$
11. $2x^2 - 8x - 3 = 0$	**12.** $2x^2 - 10x + 5 = 0$
13. $x^2 - 9x + 14 = 0$	**14.** $x^2 - 3x - 40 = 0$
15. $x^2 - 7x + 4 = 0$	**16.** $x^2 - 4x - 21 = 0$
17. $x^2 - 36 = 0$	**18.** $x^2 - 64 = 0$
19. $x^2 - 3x - 4 = 0$	**20.** $2x^2 - 7x + 3 = 0$
21. $x^2 - 6x = 16$	**22.** $x^2 - 14x + 49 = 0$
23. $0 = x^2 - 12x + 31$	**24.** $x^2 - 7x - 9 = 0$
25. $x^2 - 14x + 19 = 0$	**26.** $x^2 + 3x - 28 = 0$

Preparing for the Texas Algebra I End-of-Course Exam

The Quadratic Race, *continued*

Cards for "The Quadratic Race"

Activity for Objective 5

27. $x^2 - 16 = 0$	**28.** $0 = x^2 - 9$
29. $x^2 - 4x - 5 = 0$	**30.** $x^2 - 10x + 21 = 0$
31. $x^2 - 3x - 8 = 0$	**32.** $-2x^2 + 13x + 7 = 0$
33. $3x^2 - 13x = -10$	**34.** $4x^2 - 35x - 9 = 0$
35. $x^2 - 12x = -36$	**36.** $x^2 + 2x - 3 = 0$
37. $-x^2 - x + 6 = 0$	**38.** $2x^2 + x - 15 = 0$
39. $x^2 - 6x + 1 = 0$	**40.** $x^2 - 7x + 12 = 12$
41. $x^2 + 10x = -25$	**42.** $x^2 - 10x = 3$
43. $x^2 - 4x = 2$	**44.** $x^2 - 6x - 4 = 0$
45. $x^2 - 5x + 1 = 0$	**46.** $x^2 - 6 = 8x$
47. $x^2 - 2x - 4 = 0$	**48.** $x^2 - x - 30 = 0$
49. $x^2 + 4x = 21$	**50.** $x^2 + 2x - 15 = 0$

Four-in-a-Line

Activity for Objective 6

Number of players: 2

Materials:

- Four-in-a-Line Game Board
- Four-in-a-Line Cards
- Answer Key
- 25 playing pieces of one color
- 25 playing pieces of another color
- paper
- pencil

Directions:

The game board is positioned between the players and the shuffled game cards are placed face down next to the game board. When the players are ready, the first player draws a card and simplifies the expression written on that card. If the answer is correct, he or she is allowed to place a game piece in the first row of any column.

The next player then takes a turn, repeating the procedure except that if the player answers correctly, he or she may place a game piece not only in the first row of an empty column but also directly above a game piece in a partially filled column. From this point on, all players who answer correctly may position their pieces in this fashion.

If there is a dispute about the correct answer, the players can check the Answer Key. The game continues until one player has four pieces in a line, either horizontally, vertically, or diagonally. If a player's answer is incorrect, then that player loses his turn.

If the board is completely full or if all the cards have been used, but neither player has four pieces in a line, then the player with the most pieces on the board is the winner.

Note: Each group of players should have one copy of pages 15–17 to cut out the game cards and game board.

Four-in-a-Line, *continued*

Cards for "Four-in-a-Line"

Activity for Objective 6

1. $7x^2 + 9x^2$	**2.** $7.3x + 5.9x$
3. $(2x + 3) + (9x + 11)$	**4.** $(2x - 7) + (3x^2 - 5x - 9)$
5. $(4x^2 - x + 2) + (9x^2 - 5x - 7)$	**6.** $-7x^2 + 8x - 9 + 3x^2 + 6x + 19$
7. $(15x^2 + 9x + 19) + (13x^2 - 40)$	**8.** $12x - 17x$
9. $(5x + 8) - (8x - 17)$	**10.** $(14x - 2) - (8x - 17)$
11. $(x^2 + 9x + 3) - (7x + 8)$	**12.** $(10x^2 + 4x + 7) - (x^2 - 5x + 11)$
13. $(2x^2 - 16x - 13) - (6x^2 + 9x - 1)$	**14.** $(5x^2 + 9) - (3x^2 + 8x + 19)$
15. $5x^2 \cdot 17x$	**16.** $7x \cdot 3x^2 \cdot 2x^3$
17. $4x(3x - 14)$	**18.** $-2x^2(5x^2 - 10x + 7)$
19. $(x + 7)(x + 3)$	**20.** $(2x + 5)(x - 4)$
21. $(x + 3)(x^2 + 2x + 4)$	**22.** $\frac{1}{2}x^2 \cdot \frac{8}{9}x^3$
23. $\frac{5}{2}x^2 \cdot \frac{6}{35}x^2$	**24.** $3.5x(12x^2 + 8)$
25. $3x(x^2 - 11x + 14)$	**26.** $(x - 8)(x + 9)$

Preparing for the Texas Algebra I End-of-Course Exam

15

Four-in-a-Line, *continued*

Cards for "Four-in-a-Line"

Activity for Objective 6

27. $(3x + 6)(4x + 5)$	**28.** $(x - 2)(3x^2 - 4x + 9)$
29. $\dfrac{72x^3}{9x}$	**30.** $\dfrac{36x^2 - 18x}{6x}$
31. $\dfrac{15x^4 - 35x^3 + 65x^2}{-5x^2}$	**32.** $\dfrac{12x^3 + 48x^2 - 12x}{4x}$
33. $\dfrac{x^2 + 10x + 21}{x + 3}$	**34.** $\dfrac{2x^2 + x - 15}{x + 3}$
35. $\dfrac{3x^2 + x - 4}{3x + 4}$	**36.** $\dfrac{x^2 - 2x - 24}{x + 4}$
37. $\frac{1}{3}x^2 \cdot 39x^7$	**38.** $\dfrac{12x^2 - 2x - 2}{4x - 2}$
39. $5x^2 + 7x - 9x^2 - 12x$	**40.** $\frac{2}{3}x^3 + \frac{5}{6}x^3$
41. $\frac{1}{4}x(12x^3 - 20x^2 + 32)$	**42.** $2.3x^3 \cdot 4.1x$
43. $1.6x(7x + 4.3)$	**44.** $(5x - 9)(3x - 7)$
45. $(x + 3)^2$	**46.** $(2x - 9)^2$
47. $(x - 12)(x + 12)$	**48.** $(3x + 13)(3x - 13)$
49. $\dfrac{x^3 + 5x^2 + 11x + 10}{x + 2}$	**50.** $7(5x - 8) - 4(3x + 9)$

Four-in-a-Line, *continued*

Game Board for "Four-in-a-Line"

Activity for Objective 6

	1	2	3	4	5	6
7						
6						
5						
4						
3						
2						
1						

Solving Square-Root Equations

Activity for Objective 7 (optional)

Directions:

Solve each of the equations in the left column. Find the correct response in the right column. In the box (or boxes) at the bottom of the page, write the letter that appears after the correct answer that corresponds to the problem number.

1. $\sqrt{x + 2} = 5$ 12 – O

2. $\sqrt{2x - 1} = 9$ 375 – I

3. $\sqrt{3x} + 5 = 14$ 49 – P

4. $\sqrt{6x - 5} = 11$ 7 – R

5. $\sqrt{\frac{1}{2}x + 10} = 4$ 27 – R

6. $\sqrt{0.3x} + 7 = 10$ 41 – S

7. $\sqrt{6x + 13} = 17$ 0 – L

8. $\sqrt{\frac{3}{5}x + 19} = 34$ 25 – T

9. $14\sqrt{11x - 28} = 98$ 30 – E

10. $5\sqrt{9x} = 90$ 23 – O

11. $\frac{2}{3}\sqrt{12x} = 16$ 22 – U

12. $0.9\sqrt{4x} - 6 = 3$ 46 – O

13. $\sqrt{5x - 49} = 14$ 48 – F

14. $\frac{1}{4}\sqrt{6x + 12} = 3$ 21 – A

15. $\frac{1}{2}\sqrt{7x + 4} = 1$ 36 – Q

What did the mathematics teacher find when she dug up her tomato plants?

Problem Number:

4	13	8	15	6	1	11	2	10	14	4	3	6	9	7	5	12	2
Letter:																	

Power Play

Activity for Objective 8

Number of players: 2
Materials:
- Power Play Game Board
- 20 game tiles of one color
- 20 game tiles of another color
- Answer Key
- paper and pencil

Directions:

Place the Power Play Game Board between the two players with four game tiles (two of each color) in the middle four squares arranged as illustrated below.

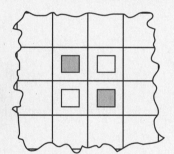

First color: Player 1

Second color: Player 2

Place the shuffled game cards face down next to the game board. When the players are ready, turn over the first card. Each player begins to simplify the expression or solve the problem. The first person to solve the problem correctly gets to place one of her game tiles on the board in the manner described below. If a player answers a problem incorrectly, then the other player is allowed to put a game tile on the board. If there is a dispute over an answer, the players can check the Answer Key to determine who will place a tile on the board.

Playing the Game Pieces:

The player placing a game tile on the board may put it on any square, provided that it is immediately to the left or right of a square that has a tile on it or immediately above or below such a square. If that player places the tile so that at least one of the other player's tiles lies between two of his or her own tiles (horizontally or vertically, not diagonally), then that player gets to replace the opponent's tiles with his or her own game tiles. Play continues until all the squares on the board have been covered. The winner is the player with the most tiles on the board.

Note: Each group of players should have one copy of pages 20–22 to cut out the game cards and game board.

Power Play, *continued*

Cards for "Power Play"

Activity for Objective 8

1. $y \cdot y \cdot y \cdot y \cdot y$	**2.** $(x^7y^9)^4$
3. $(x^3y^2)^5$	**4.** $\dfrac{(a^2b^3)^5}{(a^4b^2)^4}$
5. $xyz \cdot xy \cdot xy \cdot xyz$	**6.** $\dfrac{64c^9}{16c^9}$
7. $2x^2 \cdot 5x^3 \cdot (-3x^7)$	**8.** $\dfrac{d^{16}}{d^{31}}$
9. $\dfrac{x^7}{x^2}$	**10.** $(7j^8k^7)^3$
11. $\dfrac{5x^3y^2}{15xy^4}$	**12.** $(3x^3 \cdot x^2y^3)^3$
13. $\dfrac{20x^2y^3z^5}{10x^5y^2z^{10}}$	**14.** $(e^3f^4g^5)^3 \cdot e^2fg$
15. $6xy^2 \cdot 4x^3y^6 \cdot \frac{1}{3}x^4y^8$	**16.** $\dfrac{p^5m^9n^{18}}{p^3m^5n^7}$
17. $7x^{-4}y^{-6} \cdot 2x^5y^2$	**18.** $r^2s^4t^6 \cdot r^{-6} \cdot s^{-4}t^{-2}$
19. Write in scientific notation. $\dfrac{6000}{0.00003}$	**20.** Write in scientific notation. $\dfrac{84}{210,000}$
21. Write in scientific notation. 23,700,000,000	**22.** Write in scientific notation. 0.0000005892

Power Play, *continued*

Cards for "Power Play"

Activity for Objective 8

23. Write in scientific notation. $20{,}000 \times 4{,}300{,}000$	**24.** Write in scientific notation. 0.0008×0.000006
25. Write in scientific notation. $98{,}000{,}000{,}000{,}000$	**26.** Write in scientific notation. $0.00004 + 0.00076$
27. $y = 2x^2 + 3x + 7$ If $x = 3$, what is the value of y?	**28.** $y = x^2 - 8x - 9$ If $x = -2$, what is the value of y?
29. $y = -3x^2 + 2x - 5$ If $x = -4$, what is the value of y?	**30.** $y = x^2 + 7x - 12$ If $x = 6$, what is the value of y?
31. If the lengths of two legs of a right triangle are 14 and 48, what is the length of the hypotenuse?	**32.** Solve for x. $2x^2 = 50$
33. If the lengths of two legs of a right triangle are 9 and 12, what is the length of the hypotenuse?	**34.** Solve for n. $5n^2 = 605$
35. If the length of a leg of a right triangle is 18 and the length of the hypotenuse is 82, what is the length of the other leg?	**36.** Solve for k. $7k^2 + 13 = 76$
37. Solve for t. $6t^2 + 7t^2 = 832$	**38.** $\dfrac{w^{-3}z^{-5}}{w^4 z^{-2}}$
39. If the length of a leg of a right triangle is 12 and the length of the hypotenuse is 37, what is the length of the other leg?	**40.** A 26 foot ladder is 10 feet from the base of a vertical wall. How far up the wall will the ladder reach?
41. $r^5 s^7 t^3 \cdot r^{-3} s^6 t^{-9}$	**42.** $\dfrac{y^0 x^7}{x^3 z^5}$
43. $(0.2x^3 y^5)^2 \cdot (0.5xy^2)^3$	**44.** $\left(\dfrac{7}{12} d^4 h^8 j^2\right)^2$

Power Play, *continued*

Game Board for "Power Play"

Activity for Objective 8

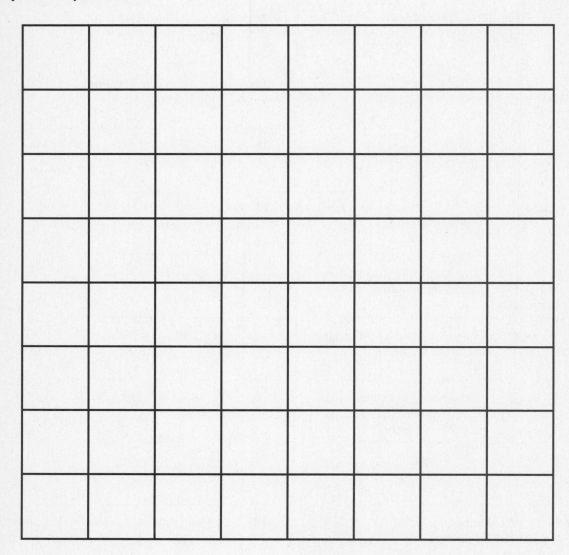

The Whimsical Baker

Activity for Objective 9

Directions:

Solve each system of equations listed below. For each solution, go to the first column at the right and find the x-coordinate of the solution. Then draw a straight line that connects it to the corresponding y-coordinate of the solution in the second column at the right. The line will go through a letter. Write that letter in the box (or boxes) below that corresponds to the problem number.

1. $2x + 3y = 8$
   $7x - 3y = 1$

2. $y = -2x - 2$
   $3x + 5y = 11$

3. $x = 7y + 5$
   $-2x + 6y = -10$

4. $-2x + 9y = -5$
   $6x - 15y = 3$

5. $7x - 2y = 12$
   $x = 0.5y + 3$

6. $4x - 5y = 3$
   $-3x + 8y = 19$

7. $3y = 2x + 27$
   $x + 4y = 3$

8. $-2x + 3y = -13$
   $0.25x - 3y = 20$

9. $5x + 4y = 8$
   $3x + 7y = -9$

10. $10x - 12y = -4$
   $16x + 28y = 29$

11. $15x + 25y = 29$
   $7.4x + 10.7y = 13$

12. $3.5x + 2.5y = 8$
   $10.5x + 5.5y = 40$

x-coordinate

0.5
1
5
7
0
4
−4
0.6
8
−9
−2
−3

Y   X
    A   I
      M
  V
    R
U
  Q
      N
  H
  K G U
    I   T
  R
      T   C D
      E   N
        Q

y-coordinate

−6
−7
2
0.8
−8
0
4
−3
−1
0.75
5
3

L   W
      P
    G   F
      O
              S
          J
        O
          N
        H
          Z

A baker had worked in the same bakery for 50 years. Upon being asked when he was going to retire, he gave the following whimsical response.

Problem Number:	I	6	3	12	8	2	7	12	4	II	10	9	5
Letter:													

What's the Probability?

Activity for Objective 10

Number of players: 2–4
Materials:
- Probability Game Board for each player
- standard deck of cards, with the face cards and jokers removed
- Probability Game Cards
- Answer Key
- paper and pencil

Directions:

Each player uses a game board. The dealer shuffles the standard deck of cards and deals two cards to each player. The players look at their two cards and place them inside the two card silhouettes on their game board so that a fraction is formed that is equal to or less than 1. The remaining playing cards are placed face down in front of the players, except for the top card, which is placed face up next to the rest of the deck.

Next, the game cards are shuffled and placed face down in front of the players. Then the first card is turned over. Each player now determines the probability of the event on the game card. The objective is to make the fraction formed by the two playing cards match the probability of the event on the game card.

The player to the left of the dealer goes first. That player may announce that the probability of the event on the game card matches the fraction on her game board, thus winning the round. Otherwise, she may pick up the playing card that is face up or draw the top card from the face-down deck. She may then either exchange that card with one of the two cards on her game board, or else discard it. If there still is no match, the process is repeated by the next player.

Play continues until one player claims to have the correct probability. If there is a dispute, then the Answer Key can be used to determine which answer is correct. The winner of the round gets two points.

To start the succeeding rounds, the player who began the preceding round reshuffles the standard deck of cards and redeals them. Then the game proceeds as before. The winner of the game is the player with the most points after all the game cards have been used.

Note: Each group of players should have one copy of pages 25–26 and multiple copies of page 27 to cut out the game cards and game boards.

Preparing for the Texas Algebra I End-of-Course Exam
Copyright © McDougal Littell Inc. All rights reserved.

What's the Probability?, *continued*

Cards for "What's the Probability?"

Activity for Objective 10

1. If today is Monday, what is the probability that tomorrow is Tuesday?	**2.** What is the probability of getting a tail when flipping a coin?
3. What is the probability of getting a number divisible by 3 when rolling a die?	**4.** In a bag there are 4 red, 24 white, and 8 green marbles. One marble is picked without looking. What is $P(\text{white})$?
5. A standard deck of cards is shuffled and a card is drawn. What is the probability of getting a diamond?	**6.** The days in a non-leap-year February are numbered on slips of paper and put in a hat. One slip is picked without looking. What is $P(\text{number} < 22)$?
7. In your pocket, there are a penny, a nickel, a dime, a quarter, and a half dollar. What is $P(\text{penny})$ if you pull one coin out?	**8.** In a bag, there are 8 red, 5 yellow, and 7 green marbles. One marble is picked. What is $P(\text{red})$?
9. Slips of paper with the letters T, E, X, A, and S are placed in a hat and one slip is picked. What is $P(\text{consonant})$?	**10.** In a cup, there are 3 quarters, 16 dimes, and 1 nickel. One coin is picked. What is $P(\text{dime})$?
11. What is the probability of getting a 2 when you roll a die?	**12.** What is the probability of not getting a 6 when rolling a die?
13. One of the names of the continents is selected at random. What is $P(\text{Europe})$?	**14.** Slips of paper with the letters C, H, I, C, A, G, and O are placed in a hat and one slip is picked. What is $P(\text{C})$?
15. Slips of paper with the letters H, O, U, S, T, O, and N are placed in a hat and one slip is picked. What is $P(\text{vowel})$?	**16.** One of the names of the continents is selected at random. What is $P(\text{name starts with A})$?

What's the Probability?, *continued*

Cards for "What's the Probability?"

Activity for Objective 10

17. Slips of paper with the names of each of the days of the week on them are placed in a box. One slip is picked. What is P(weekday)?	**18.** A dart hits a circular target with a radius of 14 cm. Within the target is another circle with an area of 168π square centimeters. What is P(dart hits smaller circle)?
19. A 1 in.-by-3 in. piece of paper is placed on a 3 in.-by-8 in. target. A dart hits the target. What is P(dart hits the piece of paper)?	**20.** In a closet, there are 3 red ties, 3 yellow ties, and 2 blue ties. One tie is picked. What is P(red tie)?
21. One marble is drawn from a bag containing 10 yellow, 3 black, 2 green, and 25 blue marbles. What is P(blue)?	**22.** Slips of paper with the integers from 1 to 16 are placed in a box. One slip is drawn. What is P(integer < 15)?
23. One of the planets in our solar system is selected at random. What is P(Earth)?	**24.** Slips of paper with the letters, W, I, S, C, O, N, S, I, and N are placed in a hat and one slip is drawn. What is P(S)?
25. An 8 in.-by-8 in. piece of paper is placed on a 12 in.-by-12 in. target. A dart hits the target. What is P(dart hits the piece of paper)?	**26.** Slips of paper with the letters M, I, L, W, A, U, K, E, and E are placed in a hat and one slip is drawn. What is P(vowel)?
27. One marble from a bag containing 2 red, 3 green, 2 blue, and 2 yellow marbles is drawn. What is P(not yellow)?	**28.** One marble from a bag containing 3 red, 5 blue, 7 white, 9 green, and 3 black marbles is drawn. What is P(not red)?
29. Each of the names of the states of the United States is written on a slip of paper and put in a box. One slip is drawn. What is P(state with a Pacific Ocean coastline)?	**30.** Slips of paper with the letters W, A, S, H, I, N, G, T, O, and N are placed in a hat and one slip is drawn. What is P(vowel)?
31. One marble from a bag containing 14 red, 4 green, and 2 blue marbles is drawn. What is P(red)?	**32.** In a dresser drawer, there are 18 white socks, 1 brown sock, and 1 black sock. One sock falls out. What is P(white sock)?

Preparing for the Texas Algebra I End-of-Course Exam

What's the Probability?, *continued*

Game Board for "What's the Probability?"

Activity for Objective 10

CARD
1

(numerator)

CARD
2

(denominator)

Concentration

Final Review Activity

Number of players: 3–5
Materials:
- Concentration Game Cards
- Concentration Answer Cards
- Answer Key
- paper
- pencil

Directions:

One of the players shuffles the game cards and the answer cards as a single deck. (Several of the cards are oversize. These may be shuffled separately.) Then the cards are placed face down in 9 rows of 10 cards each. The objective of the game is to find as many pairs of matching game cards and answer cards as possible.

The player who shuffled the cards goes first. He or she turns over a card and then a second card to try to get a matching pair. If the cards do match, then the player gets to keep the two cards and takes another turn. If they do not match, then the player turns them back face down in their original positions and his or her turn is over. Then play continues to the left in the same manner.

If a player thinks that he or she has a match and is incorrect, then the cards are returned to their original place and that player loses the next turn. The players may use pencil and paper to work out the problems. If there is a dispute, the players can check the Answer Key. Play continues until all the cards have been matched up. The winner of the game is the player with the greatest number of cards.

Note: Each group of players should have one copy of pages 29–35 to cut out the game cards and the answer cards.

Concentration, *continued*

Game Cards for "Concentration"

Final Review Activity

1. Find the range. $y = 2x - 3$ $D = \{-1, 3, 5\}$	**2.** Find the range. $y = 3x - 2$ $D = \{-1, 2, 3\}$
3. Graph the line that includes the points $(1, 3)$ and $(-1, 5)$.	**4.** Graph the line that includes the point $(1, 3)$ and that has a slope of $-\frac{1}{2}$.
5. Graph $3x + 6y = 18$.	**6.** Graph $y = -\frac{1}{3}x + 2$.
7. Graph $y - 1 = -\frac{1}{2}(x - 2)$.	**8.** Graph $y > -\frac{2}{3}x - 1$.
9. Graph $y > -\frac{1}{4}x - 1$.	**10.** Graph the system. $y = 2x + 1$ $y = -3x + 4$
11. Graph the system. $y = 3x$ $2y = 3x - 6$	**12.** Write an algebraic sentence: Five times a number increased by 18 is 28.
13. Write an algebraic sentence: Eight less than the product of some number and 5 is 27.	**14.** Write an algebraic sentence: Five times the sum of some number and 8 is 25.
15. Solve for y. $5x - 3y = 8z$	**16.** Solve for y. $2xy + 4z = 12$

Concentration, *continued*

Game Cards for "Concentration"

Final Review Activity

17. Solve the system. $2x + 3y = -2$ $x - 2y = 6$	**18.** Solve the system. $y = 4x - 9$ $\frac{1}{2}x + 2y = -1$
19. Solve the system. $3x + 2y = -1$ $2x - 3y = 8$	**20.** Solve for x. $|x + 2| = 9$
21. Solve for x. $\frac{1}{3}|x - 1| = 2$	**22.** Solve by using the quadratic formula. $2x^2 + 7x - 2 = 0$
23. Solve by using the quadratic formula. $3x^2 + 7x - 1 = 0$	**24.** Solve by using the quadratic formula. $2x^2 - 7x + 3 = 0$
25. Solve by factoring. $2x^2 - 5x - 3 = 0$	**26.** Solve by factoring. $x^2 + x - 6 = 0$
27. Simplify. $2x^2(3x - 7)$	**28.** Simplify. $2x^3 + 9x^2 + 3x^3 + 5x^2$
29. Multiply. $(2x - 3)(x + 4)$	**30.** Multiply. $(2x + 3)(x - 4)$
31. Simplify. $\dfrac{18x^5 - 36x^4}{3x^2}$	**32.** Solve. $x^2 - 19 = 30$

Preparing for the Texas Algebra I End-of-Course Exam

CLASSROOM ACTIVITIES

Concentration, *continued*

Game Cards for "Concentration"

Final Review Activity

33. Solve for x. $\sqrt{x + 3} = 3$	**34.** Simplify. $\dfrac{18x^2y^3z^4}{6xy^5z^4}$
35. Simplify. $\dfrac{24x^3y^{-4}z^0}{8xy^{-2}z^2}$	**36.** Write in scientific notation. 8,360,000,000
37. Write in scientific notation. 0.0000000836	**38.** Solve. $3x + 8 = 29$
39. Solve. $4x - 21 = 19$	**40.** Find the missing length. $x = ?$
41. Find the missing length. 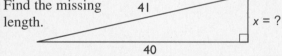 $x = ?$	**42.** Slips of paper containing the letters D, A, L, L, A, and S are placed in a hat and one slip is drawn. What is $P(\text{vowel})$?
43. One marble is drawn from a bag containing 3 blue, 4 yellow, 3 red, and 2 green marbles. What is $P(\text{red})$?	**44.** Solve. $\dfrac{x}{19} = \dfrac{20}{76}$
45. Solve by factoring. $x^2 - 121 = 0$	

Concentration, *continued*

Answer Cards for "Concentration"

Final Review Activity

1. ANSWER: $(1, -2)$	**2. ANSWER:** 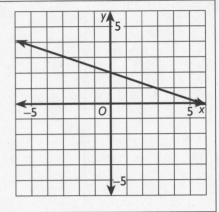
3. ANSWER: $x = -3$ or $x = 2$	**4. ANSWER:** $\dfrac{3x^2}{y^2 z^2}$
5. ANSWER: $5(x + 8) = 25$	**6. ANSWER:** $\{-5, 4, 7\}$
7. ANSWER: $x = \dfrac{-7 \pm \sqrt{61}}{6}$	**8. ANSWER:** $x = 7$
9. ANSWER: $(2, -2)$	**10. ANSWER:** 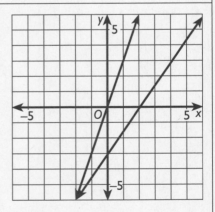
11. ANSWER: $x = \dfrac{-7 \pm \sqrt{65}}{4}$	**12. ANSWER:** $2x^2 - 5x - 12$

Concentration, *continued*

Answer Cards for "Concentration"

Final Review Activity

13. ANSWER: $(2, -1)$	**14.** ANSWER: 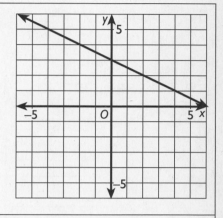
15. ANSWER: $x = 7$ or $x = -5$	**16.** ANSWER: $6x^3 - 12x^2$
17. ANSWER: $x = 8$	**18.** ANSWER: $5x - 8 = 27$
19. ANSWER: 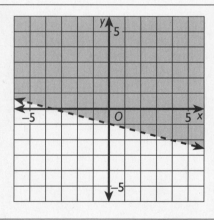	**20.** ANSWER: $x = 3$ or $x = \frac{1}{2}$
21. ANSWER: $x = 5$	**22.** ANSWER: $x = 9$
23. ANSWER: $\{-5, 3, 7\}$	**24.** ANSWER: $5x + 18 = 28$

Concentration, *continued*

Answer Cards for "Concentration"

Final Review Activity

25. ANSWER: $x = 7$ or $x = -7$	**26. ANSWER:** $x = 10$
27. ANSWER: 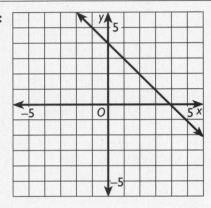	**28. ANSWER:** $6x^3 - 14x^2$
29. ANSWER: $\frac{3x}{y^2}$	**30. ANSWER:** $P = \frac{1}{3}$
31. ANSWER: 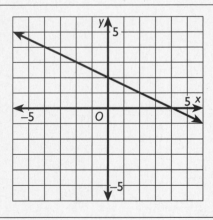	**32. ANSWER:** $y = \frac{-8z + 5x}{3}$
33. ANSWER: $5x^3 + 14x^2$	**34. ANSWER:** $x = 11$ or $x = -11$

Preparing for the Texas Algebra I End-of-Course Exam

Concentration, *continued*

Answer Cards for "Concentration"

Final Review Activity

35. ANSWER: 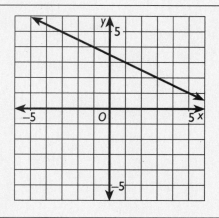	**36. ANSWER:** $2x^2 + 5x - 12$
37. ANSWER: $x = 6$	**38. ANSWER:** $P = \frac{1}{4}$
39. ANSWER: 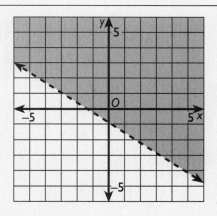	**40. ANSWER:** 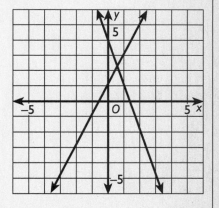
41. ANSWER: $y = \frac{6 - 2z}{x}$	**42. ANSWER:** $x = 7$ or $x = -11$
43. ANSWER: $x = 3$ or $x = -\frac{1}{2}$	**44. ANSWER:** 8.36×10^9
45. ANSWER: 8.36×10^{-8}	

EOC Practice Exam

Exam 1

1 The graph of $y = \frac{1}{2}x - 1$ is shown below.

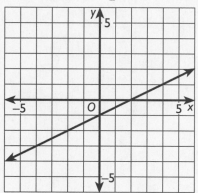

Which graph best represents $y = \frac{1}{2}x + 2$?

A

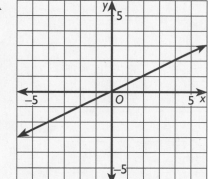

B

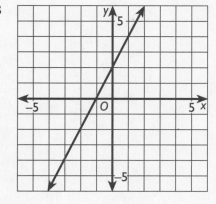

C

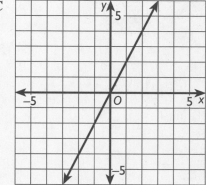

D

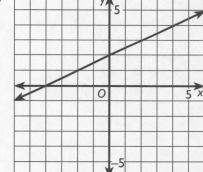

E

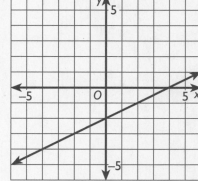

GO ON

2 Which graph best represents the equation of a line with a slope of −4 and a *y*-intercept of 3?

F

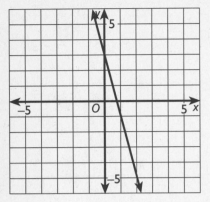

G

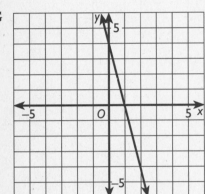

H

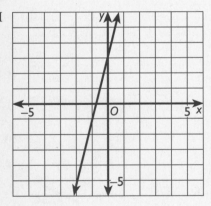

J

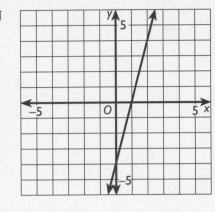

K Not Here

3 The graph of $y = \frac{3}{2}x - 3$ is shown below. Which equation best describes a line parallel to the graph of $y = \frac{3}{2}x - 3$?

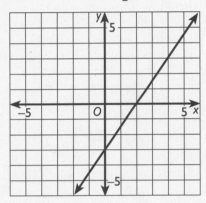

A $y = 3x - 6$

B $y = \frac{2}{3}x - 3$

C $y = -\frac{3}{2}x + 3$

D $y = \frac{3}{2}x + 2$

E $y = -\frac{2}{3}x + 1$

GO ON

Preparing for the Texas Algebra I End-of-Course Exam

4 What is the solution of this equation?

$$2(x - 3) = 3x - 11$$

Record and bubble in your answer on the answer sheet.

5 The pattern for a quilt says the finished item will be twice as long as it is wide, and it can also be made with an additional 4 inch wide border. If the width of the quilt before the border is added is w inches, which equation describes the area, A, of the finished quilt, with the border added?

F $A = (w + 8)(2w + 8)$

G $A = w(2w + 8)$

H $A = 3w + 16$

J $A = 2w(w + 8)$

K $A = (w + 4)(2w + 4)$

6 A trapezoid has two sides of length x, and bases of length $x + 3$ and $2x - 4$. Which equation describes the perimeter of the trapezoid, P, in terms of x?

A $P = 4x - 1$

B $P = 4x + 7$

C $P = 5x - 1$

D $P = 5x + 7$

E $P = x^2(3x - 1)$

7 The speed of light in a vacuum is about 300,000,000 meters per second. Which expression is another way to represent this value?

F 3×10^{10} m/s

G 3×10^9 m/s

H 3×10^8 m/s

J 3×10^7 m/s

K 3×10^6 m/s

8 Tamara and Colleen are on the math team. In the last competition, Tamara answered 5 questions more than Colleen, and together the girls answered 17 questions. How many questions did Tamara answer in the competition?

A 6

B 8

C 11

D 17

E 22

9 Janeen found a sweater on sale for $\frac{1}{3}$ off the original price. If the sale price is x, which equation could be used to find the original price, y?

F $y = x + \frac{1}{3}x$

G $y - \frac{1}{3}y = x$

H $y = x - \frac{1}{3}x$

J $y + x = \frac{1}{3}y$

K $y = x + \frac{1}{3}$

10 Over the past two weeks, Tran has been stopped by a red light at the corner of 5th and Franklin streets on 3 out of 10 morning commutes. What is the best estimate of the probability he will be stopped by the light again on his next commute?

A $\frac{1}{10}$

B $\frac{3}{10}$

C $\frac{1}{2}$

D $\frac{2}{3}$

E $\frac{7}{10}$

GO ON

Preparing for the Texas Algebra I End-of-Course Exam

11 The graph below shows the distance someone travels when biking at 10 miles per hour. The equation of the graph is $m = 10t$, where m is the distance in miles and t is the time in hours.

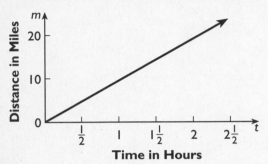

Which graph best represents the distance covered by someone biking at a rate of 15 miles an hour?

F

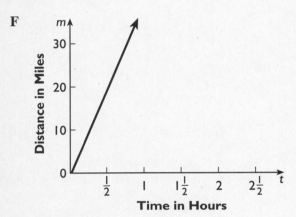

G

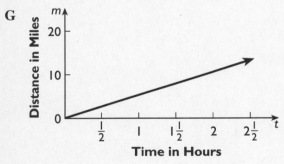

H

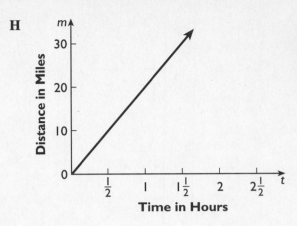

J

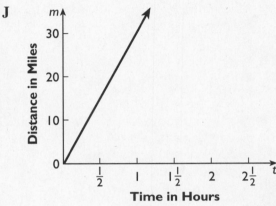

K

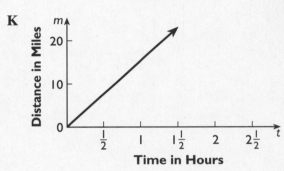

Preparing for the Texas Algebra I End-of-Course Exam

12 The graph of the system of equations

$y = x - 1$
$y = 3$

is shown at the right.

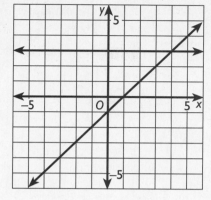

Which point is in the solution set of this system of inequalities?

$$y \leq 3$$
$$y \geq x - 1$$

A (4, 5)
B (2, –1)
C (–1, 4)
D (1, 2)
E (–2, –4)

13 Which is an equation for the line passing through the point (–1, 4) and having a slope of 2?

F $y = 2x + 6$
G $y = 2x - 3$
H $y = 2x - 6$
J $y = 2x + 3$
K $y = 2x - 7$

14 Juan has 8 coins in his pocket, all in dimes and nickels. The coins are worth 55 cents. The system of equations below describes the number of nickels, n, and dimes, d, that Juan has in his pocket. Solve the system of equations to find the number of dimes, d, that Juan has in his pocket.

$$d + n = 8$$
$$10d + 5n = 55$$

Record and bubble in your answer on the answer sheet.

15 What are the solutions to this equation?

$$x^2 + 3x - 10 = 0$$

A –5, 2
B –2, 5
C 2, 5
D –3, 10
E 3, –10

16 A rectangle with an area of $2x^2 + 8x + 6$ is modeled below using algebra tiles.

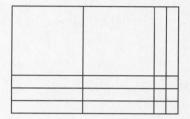

What are the dimensions of the rectangle in terms of x?

F $2x - 2$ by $x + 3$
G $2x + 2$ by $x - 3$
H $2x + 2$ by $x + 3$
J $2x + 3$ by $x + 2$
K $2x + 3$ by $x - 2$

17 Water is flowing into a circular drum so that the volume of water in the drum in t minutes is V gallons, given by the equation $V = 45 + 15t^2$. What is the volume of water in the drum after 3 minutes?

A 59 gal
B 135 gal
C 180 gal
D 540 gal
E 675 gal

18 Admission to the county fair is $7.00 for adults and $4.50 for children under 12. The Wilczeks spent $37.00 for 6 tickets. How many children under 12 were in their party?

F 2
G 3
H 4
J 5
K 6

PRACTICE EXAMS

GO ON

19 A rectangular box has a volume of 360 cubic centimeters. If its width is 6 centimeters and its height is 5 centimeters, what is its length?

   A   6 cm
   B   10 cm
   C   12 cm
   D   60 cm
   E   72 cm

20 A recipe for oatmeal cookies uses 3 cups of rolled oats for each 2 eggs. If the quantities of the recipe are increased proportionately, how many cups of rolled oats would be used with 7 eggs?

   F $4\frac{2}{3}$
   G   5
   H   8
   J   10.5
   K   12

21 The graph of the function $y = 2x$ is shown.

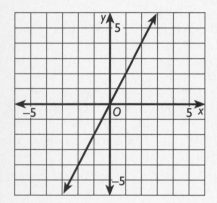

If the line is shifted down 5 units, which equation best describes the new line?

   A $y = 2x + 5$
   B $y = 5x$
   C $y = 5x + 2$
   D $y = 5x - 2$
   E $y = 2x - 5$

22. Which graph best represents the solution to the inequality $u - 4 \leq 1$?

  F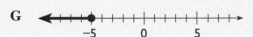

  G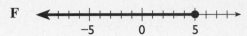

  H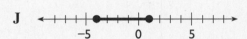

  J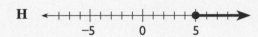

  K

23 Which equation describes the graph below?

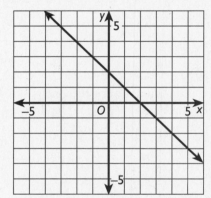

   A $y = x + 2$
   B $y = 2x + 2$
   C $y = -x + 2$
   D $y = -2x + 2$
   E $y = x + 2$

24 Find the value of c in the equation below.

$$c + \frac{c}{2} = 18$$

Record and bubble in your answer on the answer sheet.

GO ON ➡

25 An interior decorating company needs to carpet a room that is three times as long as it is wide. If the width of the carpet is w feet and the carpet costs $1.05 per square foot, which equation describes the price, P, that it will cost to carpet the room?

  A $P = 1.05(3w)$
  B $P = 1.05(4w)$
  C $P = 1.05(3w^2)$
  D $P = 1.05(4w^2)$
  E $P = w^2 + 3w + 1.05$

26 A rectangle has length $x + 8$ and width $x - 2$. Which expression gives its area?

  F $2x + 6$
  G $x^2 + 6x - 16$
  H $x^2 - 16$
  J $x^2 - 10x + 16$
  K $x^2 - 10x - 16$

27 A tall tree broke in a storm, leaving a 7 foot tall stump, and the upper portion of the tree stretched out to a point 24 feet away from the stump. How tall was the tree originally?

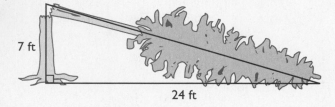

7 ft

24 ft

  A 17 ft
  B 22 ft
  C 25 ft
  D 31 ft
  E 32 ft

28 The label on a can of mixed nuts says it contains 50% peanuts. If there are 12 ounces of nuts in the can, what is the best estimate for the weight of peanuts in the can?

  F 1.2 oz
  G 4 oz
  H 6 oz
  J 8 oz
  K 12 oz

29 A company has two ways to pay for its in-state telephone calls. It can pay a flat rate of $40 per month for all calls within its area code, or $9.50 for basic service plus 25 cents per minute for each long distance call within its area code. (All such calls are made at peak rate during regular business hours.) How many minutes of long distance calls are required before the flat-rate service is less expensive?

  A 38
  B 40
  C 80
  D 122
  E 160

30 The scatter plot shows the year-to-date expenditures for miscellaneous office supplies at a real estate office. What is the best estimate for the expenditure at the end of the seventh month?

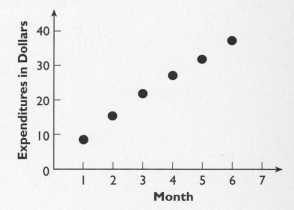

  F $30
  G $35
  H $40
  J $45
  K $50

31 What is the range of the function $f(x) = 6 - 2x^2$ over the domain $\{-3, -1, 0\}$?

  A $\{-12, 4, 6\}$
  B $\{24, 8, 6\}$
  C $\{12, 8, 6\}$
  D $\{0, 4, 6\}$
  E $\{-6, 2, 6\}$

GO ON

PRACTICE EXAMS

32 The number of grams of carbohydrate in a serving of pretzels is given by the equation $y = 22x$, where x is the weight of the serving in ounces. Which point is on the graph of this line?

F (0, 22)

G (2, 22)

H (2, 44)

J (3, 25)

K (3, 75)

33 Which is an equation for the line parallel to the graph of $y = \frac{3}{4}x - 2$?

A $y = \frac{4}{3}x - 2$

B $y = \frac{3}{4}x + 1$

C $y = -\frac{3}{4}x - 2$

D $y = 3x + 4$

E $y = -\frac{4}{3}x + 2$

34 What is the value of x in this equation?

$$3x = 2(x + 4)$$

Record and bubble in your answer on the answer sheet.

35 What are the solutions to this equation?

$$2x^2 - x - 15 = 0$$

F 1, 15

G −1, −15

H $-\frac{5}{2}$, 3

J $\frac{5}{2}$, −3

K 1, $\frac{15}{2}$

36 A rectangle with an area of $3x^2 + 10x + 3$ is modeled below using algebra tiles.

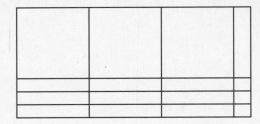

Which expression gives the correct factors of $3x^2 + 10x + 3$?

A $(3x + 1)(x + 3)$

B $(3x + 3)(x + 1)$

C $3x(x - 3)$

D $(3x - 1)(x + 3)$

E $(3x + 1)(x - 3)$

37 Suppose the height to which a plant grows is related to the amount of rainfall it receives by the equation $h = 8x - \frac{1}{2}x^2$, where h is the height in inches and x is the amount of rainfall in inches. Selena wants to discover how much rain is required to produce plants at least 24 inches tall. Which of the strategies would help her find a solution?

F Factor $8x - \frac{1}{2}x^2$.

G Factor $\frac{1}{2}x^2 - 8x + 24$.

H Divide both sides of the equation by 8.

J Subtract $8x$ from both sides of the equation.

K Add 24 to both sides of the equation.

GO ON

PRACTICE EXAMS

38 If $(-2, y)$ is a solution of the equation $3x + 2y = 1$, what is the value of y?

    A $-\dfrac{5}{2}$

    B $\dfrac{7}{2}$

    C $\dfrac{9}{2}$

    D $\dfrac{13}{2}$

    E   14

39 Pat walks at 4 miles per hour and jogs at 6 miles per hour each day for exercise. One week, she went 17 miles and spent a total of 3 hours exercising. How much time did she spend walking?

    F   0.5 h

    G   1.5 h

    H   2 h

    J   2.5 h

    K   3.5 h

40 Natalie interviewed 25 students in the lunch room and found that 9 of them planned to vote for Marie DeForge for student council president. If there are 1019 students at her school, about how many of them would you expect to vote for Marie in the election?

    A   41

    B   250

    C   370

    D   400

    E   650

The following questions are optional in terms of assessment due to the recent modifications to the End-of-Course Exam objectives for Algebra 1. The following section contains questions involving absolute value from Objective 5 and questions pertaining to Objective 7.

41 What are the solutions to this equation?

$$|u - 3| = 4$$

    F $-7, 7$

    G $-1, 7$

    H $-1, 1$

    J $-7, 1$

    K $1, 7$

42 Together, Jan and Jerry can mow a lawn in 2 hours. By herself, Jan can mow the lawn in 3 hours. The equation below can be used to determine h, the number of hours Jerry would require to mow the lawn by himself.

$$\frac{2}{3} + \frac{2}{h} = 1$$

How many hours would it take Jerry to mow the lawn?

    A   2

    B   3

    C   4

    D   6

    E   8

43 What are the solutions to this equation?

$$|2y| + 5 = 9$$

    F $-1, 1$

    G $-2, 2$

    H $-4, 4$

    J $-7, 7$

    K $-14, 14$

PRACTICE EXAMS

GO ON

44 The Hoy family made a trip of 459 miles by car. They averaged 51 miles per hour on the trip. The equation below can be used to determine h, the number of hours they traveled.

$$\frac{459}{h} = 51$$

How many hours did their trip take?

A 4 h
B 6 h
C 8 h
D 9 h
E 10 h

45 The water level of a water storage tank should remain at approximately 200 ft. The person who monitors this level uses the inequality $|l - 200| \leq 20$ to describe the acceptable water level ranges, l, in feet. What is the acceptable range of water levels?

F $l \leq 180$ ft or $l \geq 220$ ft
G 180 ft $< l < 220$ ft
H 180 ft $\leq l \leq 220$ ft
J 180 ft $\geq l \geq 220$ ft
K $l \leq 220$ ft

46 What is the value of s in this equation?

$$4 + \sqrt{s - 2} = 7$$

A 2
B 4
C 7
D 9
E 11

47 What are the solutions to this equation?

$$|v - 16| = 31$$

F −47, 47
G −15, 47
H 15, 31
J 15, 47
K 31, 47

48 What is the value of x in this equation?

$$\sqrt{x} = 8$$

A 2
B 4
C 16
D 64
E 100

EOC Practice Exam

Exam 2

1 If $(x, -3)$ is a solution of the equation $2x - y = 6$, what is the value of x?

Record and bubble in your answer on the answer sheet.

2 A rectangular box has a volume of 480 in.^{3}. If its width is 4 in. and its height is 8 in., what is the number of inches in its length?

Record and bubble in your answer on the answer sheet.

3 What is the solution of this equation?

$$4x + 5 = 3(x + 2)$$

Record and bubble in your answer on the answer sheet.

4 A kite has two long sides of length $2x + 3$ and two shorter sides each of length $x + 7$. Which equation describes the perimeter, P, of the kite in terms of x?

A $P = 3x + 10$
B $P = 6x + 20$
C $P = 6x + 10$
D $P = 4x + 17$
E $P = 2x^2 + 17x + 21$

5 Henry read 12 books last month. He read 4 more fiction books than nonfiction books. Which equation can be used to find the number of fiction books, f, he read last month?

F $(f - 4) + f = 12$
G $f + (f + 4) = 12$
H $4f = 12$
J $f + 4 = 12$
K $f - 4 = 12$

6 Mia bought refreshments for a group of friends at the movie theater. A bag of nuts costs \$1.25 and a cup of popcorn costs \$2.00. She purchased 7 items for a total of \$9.00. Which system of equations will determine the number of bags of nuts, b, and cups of popcorn, c, that she bought?

A $b + c = 7$
   $1.25b + 2c = 9$

B $b + c = 7$
   $125b + 2c = 9$

C $b + c = 7$
   $3.25(b + c) = 9$

D $1.25b + 2c = 7$
   $b + c = 9$

E $1.25c + 2b = 9$
   $b = 7 - c$

7 The Taylors have a square area rug in their living room. The room is 2 feet wider and 6 feet longer than the rug. If the rug is x feet long on each side, which equation describes the area, A, of their living room?

F $A = (x + 2)(x + 6)$
G $A = 2x + 8$
H $A = x(x + 8)$
J $A = x^2 + 12$
K $A = (x - 2)(x - 6)$

8 What are the solutions to this equation?

$$x^2 - 3x - 10 = 0$$

A $-2, 5$
B $-5, 2$
C $-3, -10$
D $3, 10$
E $2, 5$

GO ON

9 A rectangle with an area of $2x^2 + 7x + 5$ is modeled below using algebra tiles.

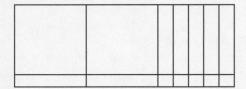

What are the dimensions of the rectangle in terms of x?

F $2x + 5$ by $x - 1$
G $2x - 5$ by $x + 1$
H $2x + 5$ by $x + 1$
J $2x + 1$ by $x + 5$
K $2x - 1$ by $x + 5$

10 A rectangle has length $x + 6$ and width $x - 3$. Which expression gives its area?

A $x^2 + 3x - 18$
B $2x + 3$
C $x^2 - 18$
D $x^2 + 3$
E $x^2 - 3x - 18$

11 A rectangle with an area of $3x^2 + 7x + 2$ is modeled below using algebra tiles.

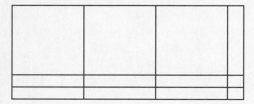

Which expression gives the correct way to factor $3x^2 + 7x + 2$?

F $(3x + 2)(x + 1)$
G $(3x - 1)(x + 2)$
H $3x(x - 2)$
J $(3x + 1)(x + 2)$
K $(3x + 1)(x - 2)$

12 You need a 20-cent stamp to mail a postcard and a 32-cent stamp to mail a letter. Which inequality can be used to determine the possible cost of postage, p, for sending 6 pieces of mail?

A $6(0.20) \le p \le 6(0.32)$
B $0.20 \le 6p \le 0.32$
C $p \ge 6(0.20 + 0.32)$
D $p \le 6(0.20 + 0.32)$
E $6(0.32) \le p \le 6(0.20)$

13 What are the solutions to this equation?

$$2x^2 + x - 21 = 0$$

F $x = -\frac{7}{2}$ or $x = 3$
G $x = -3$ or $x = \frac{7}{2}$
H $x = 2$ or $x = 21$
J $x = 3$ or $x = \frac{7}{2}$
K $x = 3$ or $x = 7$

14 Will wants to build a fence extending from the back of his house and surrounding his back yard. He intends to use a total of 30 feet of fencing for three sides of his rectangular back yard and his house as the fourth side. If y represents the length of the sides perpendicular to the house, which equation describes the area, A, of his back yard?

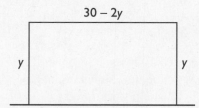

A $A = 60 - 4y$
B $A = y(30 - 2y)$
C $A = 2y(30 - 2y)$
D $A = y^2 + (30 - 2y)$
E $A = 30 + 2y$

GO ON

Preparing for the Texas Algebra I End-of-Course Exam

15 Walter and Ramon are competing on a game show. Together, they answered questions correctly 22 times. Ramon's score was 8 less than twice Walter's score. How many questions did Ramon answer correctly?

F   10
G   12
H   14
J   16
K   18

16 Admission to a concert by the college orchestra was $6.50 for nonstudents and $3.00 for students. A group of students and nonstudents attended the concert and paid a total of $44.50 for their tickets. If there were 9 people in the group, how many were students?

A   2
B   3
C   4
D   5
E   7

17 A 13 foot ramp is set up so that one end reaches the edge of a stage 5 feet above ground level. How far away from the foot of the stage does the bottom of the ramp reach?

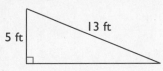

F   8 ft
G   10 ft
H   12 ft
J   13 ft
K   18 ft

18 The national debt of the U.S. government was approximately $4,071,000,000,000 at the end of 1992. Which expression is another correct representation of this value?

A 4.071×10^{14}
B 4.071×10^{13}
C 4.071×10^{12}
D 4.071×10^{9}
E 4.071×10^{8}

19 Carl found a pair of hiking boots on sale for 25% off the original price. If the sale price is x, which equation could be used to find the original price, y?

F $y = x + \frac{1}{4}x$
G $y - \frac{1}{4}y = x$
H $y = x - \frac{1}{4}x$
J $y + x = \frac{1}{4}y$
K $y = x + \frac{1}{4}$

20 A ball is dropped from the top of a building. Its height above the ground t seconds later is given by the equation $h = 90 - 4.9t^2$, where h is the height in meters. What is the height above the ground of the ball after 3 seconds?

A   45.9 m
B   60.6 m
C   75.3 m
D   515.4 m
E   765.9 m

21 An annual membership at a fitness center costs $225. Without membership, each use of the facility costs an extra $3.00 above what a member would pay. How many visits would you have to make to the center for the cost of membership to be less expensive than paying the visitor's fee?

F   36
G   70
H   76
J   125
K   222

GO ON

PRACTICE EXAMS

22 In the last 6 games, Alicia has had 20 turns at bat. She hit a single 7 times. What is the best estimate of the probability she will hit a single the next time she is at bat?

A $\frac{1}{7}$

B $\frac{1}{6}$

C $\frac{3}{10}$

D $\frac{7}{20}$

E $\frac{6}{7}$

23 A recipe for making modeling dough requires 2 tablespoons of vegetable oil for each cup of salt. How much vegetable oil would be needed to mix with 2 cups of salt?

F 2.5 tablespoons
G 4 tablespoons
H 8 tablespoons
J 9 tablespoons
K 10 tablespoons

24 The scatter plot shows the sales at a new company over the last several quarters.

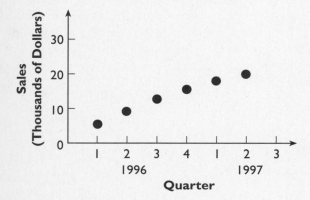

Which is the best estimate for the expected sales in the third quarter of 1997?

A $17,000
B $20,000
C $23,000
D $27,000
E $30,000

25 For exercise, Tod bicycles at 15 miles per hour and runs at 8 miles per hour. One week, he covered a total of 57 miles in 4.5 hours of exercise. How much time did he spend bicycling?

F 1 h
G 1.5 h
H 2 h
J 2.5 h
K 3 h

26 Suppose the total sales receipts for a book is related to the price of the book by the equation $S = 40 + 31x - x^2$, where S is the total sales receipts in thousands of dollars and x is the price in dollars. Which of the strategies would help decide the lowest price for earning at least $280,000 from the book?

A Factor $40 + 31x - x^2$.
B Factor $x^2 - 31x + 240$.
C Divide both sides of the equation by 31.
D Divide both sides of the equation by 40.
E Add 280 to both sides of the equation.

27 Kinta counted 7 out-of-state license plates in the first row of 50 cars parked at the county fair. If there are 408 cars in the lot, about how many of them would you expect to have out-of-state license plates?

F 28
G 35
H 40
J 50
K 57

GO ON

28 The label on a carton of low-fat ice cream says it has 50% less fat than the company's regular ice cream. If a serving of the low-fat ice cream has 30 calories from fat, how many calories from fat are in a serving of the regular ice cream?

   A   15 Cal
   B   45 Cal
   C   60 Cal
   D   75 Cal
   E   90 Cal

29 Which graph best represents the equation of a line with a slope of −3 and a *y*-intercept of 2?

F
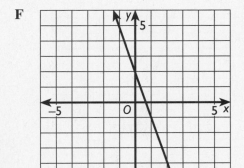

G
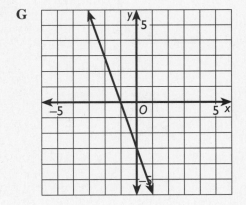

H
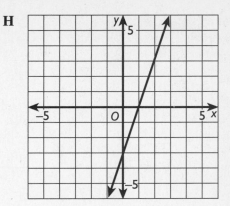

J
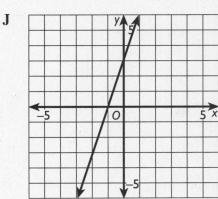

K
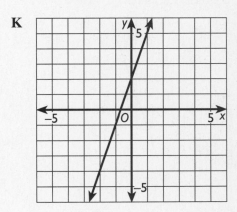

GO ON

30 The graph of the system of equations

$y = 2x + 1$
$x = 4$

is shown at the right.

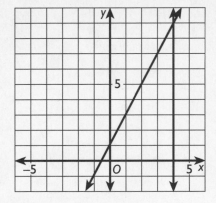

Which point is in the solution set of this system of inequalities?

$x \leq 4$
$y \geq 2x + 1$

A (2, 2)
B (2, 5)
C (−2, 3)
D (5, 2)
E (5, 12)

31 The graph of $y = 3x$ is shown below.

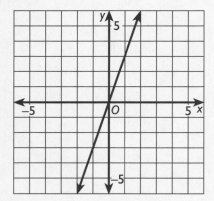

Which graph best represents $y = 3x - 3$?

F

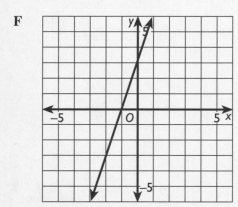

G

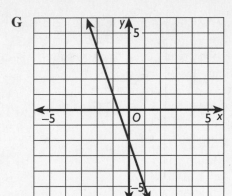

H

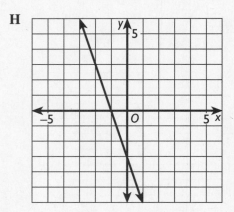

J

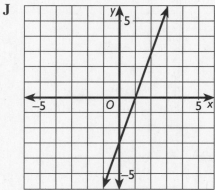

K Not Here

GO ON

Preparing for the Texas Algebra I End-of-Course Exam
Copyright © McDougal Littell Inc. All rights reserved.

32 The graph below shows the distance covered by someone who is walking at a rate of 4 miles per hour. The equation is $d = 4h$, where d is the distance in miles and h is the number of hours walked.

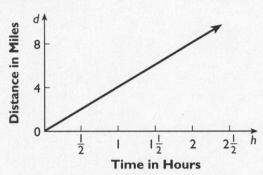

Which graph best represents the distance covered by someone walking at a rate of 5 miles per hour?

A

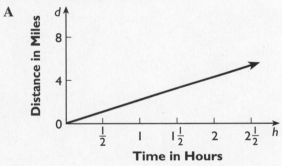

B

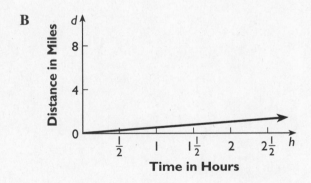

C

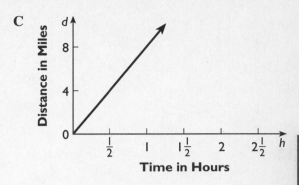

D

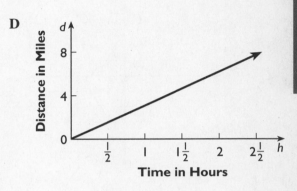

E

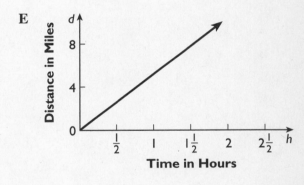

33 What is the range of the function
$f(x) = 5 - 3x^2$ over the domain $\{-2, -1, 0\}$?

   F $\{-7, 2, 5\}$
   G $\{17, 8, 5\}$
   H $\{8, 2, 5\}$
   J $\{1, 4, 25\}$
   K $\{11, 8, 5\}$

34 The graph of $y = \frac{2}{5}x + 1$ is shown below.

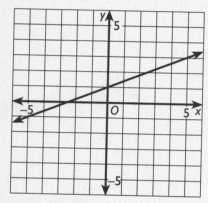

Which equation best describes a line parallel
to the graph of $y = \frac{2}{5}x + 1$?

   A $y = 2x + 5$

   B $y = \frac{5}{2}x + 1$

   C $y = -\frac{2}{5}x - 1$

   D $y = -\frac{5}{2}x + 1$

   E $y = \frac{2}{5}x - 4$

35 Which graph best represents the solution to
this inequality?

$$v + 2 \geq 6$$

F

G

H

J

K

36 Which is an equation for the line passing
through the point $(2, -2)$ and having a slope
of 3?

   A $y = 3x - 8$
   B $y = 3x + 8$
   C $y = 3x$
   D $y = 3x - 4$
   E $y = 3x + 4$

37 Which equation describes the graph shown?

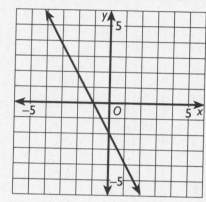

   F $y = x - 2$
   G $y = 2x - 2$
   H $y = -x - 2$
   J $y = -2x - 2$
   K $y = x - 2$

GO ON

38 The graph of the function $y = \frac{2}{3}x$ is shown below. If the line is shifted up 4 units, which equation below best describes the new line?

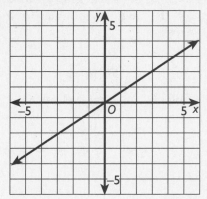

A $y = \frac{2}{3}x - 4$

B $y = \frac{2}{3}x + 4$

C $y = 4x$

D $y = \frac{2}{3}(x + 4)$

E $y = 4x + \frac{2}{3}$

39 The number of grams of sugar in one serving of a breakfast cereal is given by the equation $y = 15x$, where x is the weight of the serving in ounces. Which point is on the graph of this line?

F (0, 15)

G (2, 15)

H (2, 30)

J (3, 18)

K (3, 30)

40 Which is an equation for the line that has a slope of -4 and that contains the point (0, 5)?

A $y = -4x$

B $y = -4x + 5$

C $y = -4(x + 5)$

D $y = \frac{1}{4}x - 5$

E $y = -\frac{1}{4}x + 5$

The following questions are optional in terms of assessment due to the recent modifications to the End-of-Course Exam objectives for Algebra 1. The following section contains questions involving absolute value from Objective 5 and questions pertaining to Objective 7.

41 What is the value of x in this equation?

$$\frac{3}{4} + \frac{3}{x} = 1$$

F 3

G 4

H 9

J 12

K 15

42 What is the value of x in this equation?

$$-5 + 3\sqrt{x} = 7$$

A $\frac{5}{3}$

B 3

C 4

D 8

E 16

43 What are the solutions to this equation?

$$|p + 2| = 5$$

F $-7, 3$

G $-3, 7$

H $3, 7$

J $-7, 7$

K $-3, 3$

44 What are the solutions to this equation?

$$|4x| - 2 = 10$$

A $-12, 12$

B $-4, 4$

C $-3, 3$

D $-2, 2$

E $-1, 1$

PRACTICE EXAMS

GO ON

45 What is the value of t in this equation?

$$\sqrt{t-3} + 6 = 10$$

   F 3
   G 4
   H 7
   J 16
   K 19

46 What is the value of x in this equation?

$$\sqrt{x} = 10$$

   A 5
   B 20
   C 25
   D 100
   E 1000

47 A school decides that its class trips for the year should be to places about 1 hour away. The inequality $|t - 60| < 20$ describes the acceptable range of trip times, t, in minutes. Which is the range of trip times for the class trips?

   F $t > 40$ min
   G 40 min $< t < 80$ min
   H 40 min $\le t \le 80$ min
   J $t < 80$ min
   K $t \le 80$ min

48 What are the solutions to this equation?

$$|6x| + 3 = 21$$

   A −9, 9
   B −6, 6
   C −4, 4
   D −3, 3
   E −2, 2

PRACTICE EXAMS

Preparing for the Texas Algebra I End-of-Course Exam

Practice for Objective 1

OBJECTIVE 1 **The student will demonstrate an understanding of the characteristics of graphing in problems involving real-world and mathematical situations.**

Instructional Target: Describe the domains and ranges of various functions and relations

A **function** pairs each input value x with a unique output value y. The **domain** of a function is the set of permissible input values. The **range** of a function is the set of all output values.

The **function notation** $y = f(x)$, read "y equals f of x," tells you that y is a function of x. If there is a rule relating y to x, such as $y = 3x + 1$, then you can also write $f(x) = 3x + 1$.

Example: What is the range of the function $f(x) = 3x - 5$ when the domain is $\{2, 4, 6\}$?

Solution: x is the input variable and y is the output variable.

When $x = 2$: $\quad f(x) = 3x - 5$
$\qquad\qquad\quad f(2) = 3(2) - 5 \quad$ Replace x with 2.
$\qquad\qquad\quad f(2) = 6 - 5 \qquad$ Multiply.
$\qquad\qquad\quad f(2) = 1 \qquad\quad$ Subtract.

When $x = 4$: $\quad f(x) = 3x - 5$
$\qquad\qquad\quad f(4) = 3(4) - 5 \quad$ Replace x with 4.
$\qquad\qquad\quad f(4) = 12 - 5 \qquad$ Multiply.
$\qquad\qquad\quad f(4) = 7 \qquad\quad$ Subtract.

When $x = 6$: $\quad f(x) = 3x - 5$
$\qquad\qquad\quad f(6) = 3(6) - 5 \quad$ Replace x with 6.
$\qquad\qquad\quad f(6) = 18 - 5 \qquad$ Multiply.
$\qquad\qquad\quad f(6) = 13 \qquad\quad$ Subtract.

The range is $\{1, 7, 13\}$.

Practice Exercises:

Find the range of the functions with the given domain, D.

1. $f(x) = x \quad D = \{6, 7, 8\}$

2. $f(x) = -2x + 3 \quad D = \{0, 4, 8\}$

3. $f(x) = x^2 + 2 \quad D = \{1, 3, 5\}$

4. $f(x) = \dfrac{1}{x - 1} \quad D = \{-2, 0, 2\}$

5. $f(x) = 5x - 4 \quad D = \{-3, -2, -1\}$

6. $f(x) = -5x + 4 \quad D = \{-3, 4, 7, 10\}$

7. $f(x) = \dfrac{1}{x^2} \quad D = \{-1, 1, 4\}$

8. $f(x) = 8 - 2x \quad D = \{10, 20, 30, 40, 50\}$

9. $f(x) = 3x^2 + 1 \quad D = \{-1, 0, 5\}$

10. $f(x) = \dfrac{1}{x^2 - 1} \quad D = \{-3, 0, 3, 7\}$

11. $f(x) = |-3x + 5| \quad D = \{-3, -2, -1, 0\}$

12. $f(x) = |2x - 4| \quad D = \{3, 4, 5, 6\}$

PRACTICE WORKSHEETS

Example: Which of the following relations represents a function?

      a. {(1, 2), (2, 4), (3, 6), (4, 4)}   **b.** {(−2, 3), (−1, 0), (−1, 6)}

Solution: **a.** This relation represents a function. For each input value, there is only one output value.

      b. This relation does not represent a function. For the input value −1, there are two different output values, 0 and 6.

Which of the following relations represents a function?

13. {(1, 3), (2, 6), (3, 9), (4, 11)}

14. {(−1, 2), (−2, 4), (−3, 6), (−1, −2)}

15. {(−2, 3), (−4, 4), (−6, 5), (8, 6)}

16. {(0, 4), (2, 4), (4, 4), (6, 4)}

17. {(4, 0), (4, 2), (4, 4), (4, 6)}

18. {(0, 5), (2, 6), (4, 7), (6, 8)}

19. {(−1, −8), (−2, −8), (−8, −2), (−8, −1)}

20. {(0, −10), (1, −5), (2, 0), (3, 3)}

Example: Which of the following tables represents a function?

a.

Age (years)	Weight (pounds)
10	75
11	78
11	84
12	76
13	85

b.

x	x^3
−1	−1
0	0
1	1
2	8
3	27

Solution: **a.** This table does not represent a function. For the input value age 11, there are two different output values, 78 pounds and 84 pounds.

      b. This table represents a function. For each input value of x, there is only one corresponding output value of x^3.

Which of the following tables represents a function?

21.

x	x^4
−1	1
0	0
1	1
2	16
3	81

22.

Height (inches)	Age (years)
55	13
64	14
66	15
64	16
70	18

23.

Radius	Area
2	4π
3	9π
4	16π
5	25π
6	36π

PRACTICE WORKSHEETS

Preparing for the Texas Algebra I End-of-Course Exam

Instructional Target: Identify the effects of simple parameter changes on the graphs of relations and linear, quadratic, and absolute value functions

An equation of the form $y = mx + b$ has a graph that is a line. The slope of the line is given by m and the y-intercept of the line is given by b. Changing m changes how "steep" the line will be, and changing b shifts the line either up or down.

Example: The graph at the right shows the amount a person earns working at a rate of $5 per hour. The slope is 5. Since the line passes through the origin, the y-intercept is 0. So, the equation is $a = 5h$.

Draw a graph that shows the amount a person earns working at a rate of $7 per hour.

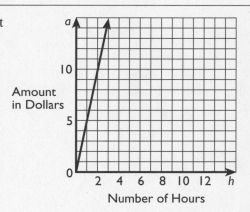

Solution: The equation is $a = 7h$. This line has a slope of 7 and a y-intercept of 0. The graph of this line is steeper than the graph of the line given above.

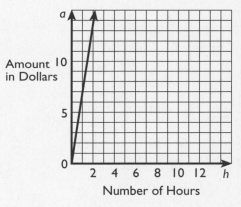

Draw the graph that shows the amount a person earns working at the rate shown.

24. $6 per hour   **25.** $8 per hour

26. $10 per hour   **27.** $6.50 per hour

PRACTICE WORKSHEETS

Example: The graph of the line $y = x - 4$ is shown at the right. If the line is shifted 5 units up, what is the equation of the new line?

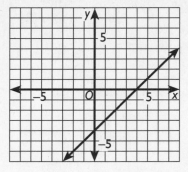

Solution: The graph of the new line is shown at the right. It has a y-intercept of 1 and its equation is $y = x + 1$.

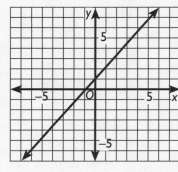

The graph of $y = \frac{2}{3}x + 2$ is given. Give the equation for the new line if the given line is shifted as shown.

28. 6 units up

29. 5 units down

30. 3 units up

31. 7 units down

32. 4 units down

33. 10 units up

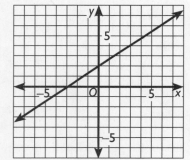

PRACTICE WORKSHEETS

Cumulative Practice for Objective 1

1. The graph of $y = -3x$ is shown at the right. Which of the graphs below best represents $y = -3x - 2$?

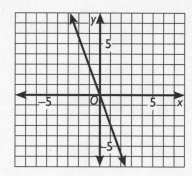

A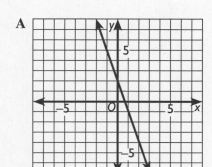

B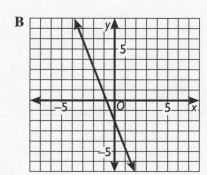

C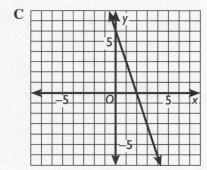

D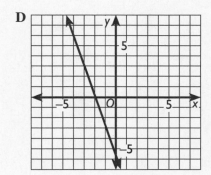

E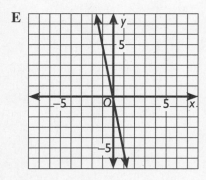

2. The graph at the right shows the distance a person travels walking at a rate of 3 miles per hour.

An equation of the line is

$$d = 3t,$$

where d is the distance in miles and t is the time in hours. Which of the graphs below best represents the distance a person travels walking at a rate of 4 miles per hour?

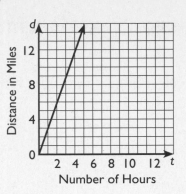

A

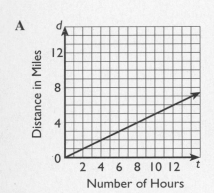

B

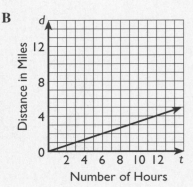

C

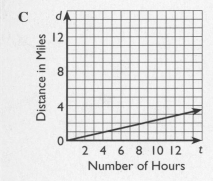

D

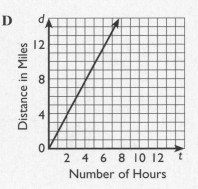

E

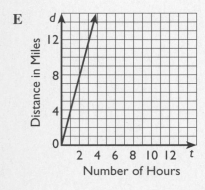

PRACTICE WORKSHEETS

3. What is the range of the function $f(x) = x - 5$ when the domain is $\{2, 7, 9\}$?

    A $\{-3, 2, 4\}$

    B $\{2, 3, 4\}$

    C $\{-4, -3, -2\}$

    D $\{7, 12, 14\}$

    E $\{-7, 12, 14\}$

4. The graph of $y = \frac{3}{4}x$ is shown at the right. If the line is shifted 3 units up, which equation best describes the new line?

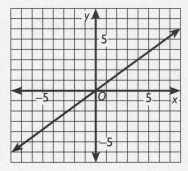

    A $y = \frac{3}{4}(x + 3)$

    B $y = \frac{3}{4}(x - 3)$

    C $y = \frac{3}{4}x + 3$

    D $y = \frac{3}{4}x - 3$

    E $y = 3x + \frac{3}{4}$

5. What is the range of the function $f(x) = x^2 + 4$ when the domain is $\{-3, -2, -1\}$?

    A $\{-2, 0, 2\}$

    B $\{-5, 0, 3\}$

    C $\{-10, 5, 8\}$

    D $\{5, 8, 13\}$

    E $\{-13, -8, -5\}$

PRACTICE WORKSHEETS

Practice for Objective 2

OBJECTIVE 2 The student will graph problems involving real-world and mathematical situations.

Instructional Target: Graph a line given its characteristics or its equation

There are several forms for the equation of a line. Here are three of them.

$y = mx + b$ slope-intercept form

$y - y_1 = m(x - x_1)$ point-slope form

$Ax + By = C$ standard form, or general form

The line $y = \frac{2}{3}x - 4$ is in slope-intercept form. The slope is $\frac{2}{3}$. The y-intercept is -4, which means that the line passes through the point $(0, -4)$.

The line $y - 3 = \frac{3}{4}(x + 1)$ is in point-slope form. The slope is $\frac{3}{4}$ and the line passes through the point $(-1, 3)$.

Example: Graph the equation $y - 1 = -\frac{3}{2}(x + 1)$.

Solution: This equation is in point-slope form. The slope is $-\frac{3}{2}$ and a point on the line is $(-1, 1)$. The slope is $\frac{\text{vertical change}}{\text{horizontal change}}$, which is $-\frac{3}{2}$ in this example. A vertical change of -3 means move down 3 units and a horizontal change of 2 means move to the right 2 units.

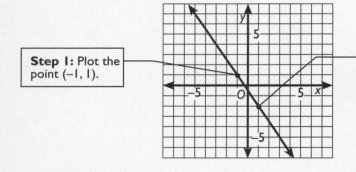

Step 1: Plot the point $(-1, 1)$.

Step 2: From the point $(-1, 1)$, move down 3 units and to the right 2 units to get another point on the line, $(1, -2)$ in this example.

Practice Exercises:

Graph each equation.

1. $y - 3 = \frac{3}{4}(x + 1)$

2. $y = -\frac{5}{3}x + 4$

3. $y - 1 = -\frac{2}{3}(x - 5)$

4. $y = \frac{5}{4}x - 8$

5. $y + 4 = 3(x - 2)$

6. $y = -2x + 6$

Graph each line with the given characteristics.

7. has slope $-\frac{2}{5}$ and passes through $(-3, 5)$

8. has slope $\frac{1}{5}$ and passes through $(3, -2)$

9. passes through $(2, 5)$ and $(-2, -5)$

10. passes through $(-3, 7)$ and $(5, -2)$

11. has slope $\frac{5}{3}$ and y-intercept -6

12. has slope $\frac{1}{7}$ and y-intercept 4

Example: Graph the equation $5x + 3y = 15$.

Solution: This is the equation of a line in standard form. One method for graphing this equation is to rewrite it in slope-intercept form first. Another method is to find two points on the line using substitution. The second method is shown here.

Substitute 0 for x.
$5(0) + 3y = 15$
$3y = 15$
$y = 5$

Substitute 0 for y.
$5x + 3(0) = 15$
$5x = 15$
$x = 3$

The two points are $(0, 5)$ and $(3, 0)$.
Plot the points and draw the line.

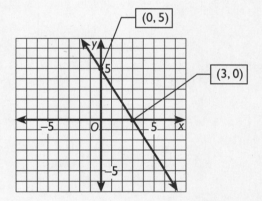

Graph each equation.

13. $4x - 2y = 8$

14. $5x + y = -10$

15. $x - 7y = 7$

16. $3x - 2y = 12$

17. $-6x + 3y = 9$

18. $-4x - 3y = 24$

19. $-8x + y = -8$

20. $-x + 3y = -6$

PRACTICE WORKSHEETS

Instructional Target: Graph linear inequalities in one or two variables

The solution for a linear inequality in one variable is graphed on the number line. The solution for a linear inequality in two variables is graphed on the coordinate plane.

Example: Graph the solution of each inequality.

    a. $2 - 3x > x - 6$ **b.** $x - 3 \geq -2$

Solution: **a.** Solve the inequality for x.

$$2 - 3x > x - 6$$

$2 - 3x - 2 > x - 6 - 2$ Subtract 2 from both sides.

$-3x > x - 8$ Simplify.

$-3x - x > x - 8 - x$ Subtract x from both sides.

$-4x > -8$ Simplify.

$\dfrac{-4x}{-4} < \dfrac{-8}{-4}$ Divide both sides by -4
and reverse the inequality symbol.

$x < 2$ Simplify.

Graph all numbers less than 2.

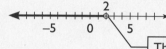

The number 2 is not part of the solution, so use an open circle.

b. Solve the inequality for x.

$$x - 3 \geq -2$$

$x - 3 + 3 \geq -2 + 3$ Add 3 to both sides.

$x \geq 1$ Simplify.

Graph all numbers greater than or equal to 1.

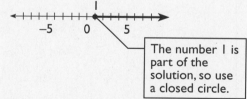

The number 1 is part of the solution, so use a closed circle.

Graph the solution of each inequality.

21. $3x - 2 < x + 4$ **22.** $5 - x \geq 3 + x$

23. $3 - 2x < 8$ **24.** $3x + 5 \leq -10$

25. $1 - 5x > 20$ **26.** $7x > 14$

27. $7 - x \geq 7$ **28.** $8 < 3x - 7$

29. $13 > x + 9$ **30.** $2x - 8 \leq 0$

31. $1 - 5x < 2x + 7$ **32.** $3 + 4x > -x - 2$

Example: Graph the solution of $2x - 3y > 6$.

Solution: **Step 1:** Solve $2x - 3y > 6$ for y.

$$2x - 3y > 6$$

$$2x - 3y - 2x > 6 - 2x \qquad \text{Subtract } 2x \text{ from both sides.}$$

$$-3y > 6 - 2x \qquad \text{Combine like terms.}$$

$$\frac{-3y}{-3} < \frac{6}{-3} - \frac{2x}{-3} \qquad \begin{array}{l}\text{Divide both sides by } -3 \text{ and}\\ \text{reverse the inequality symbol.}\end{array}$$

$$y < -2 + \frac{2}{3}x \qquad \text{Simplify.}$$

Step 2: Graph the line $y = -2 + \frac{2}{3}x$, or $y = \frac{2}{3}x - 2$.

The slope is $\frac{2}{3}$ and the y-intercept is -2.

Step 3: Shade all points for which *y is less than* $\frac{2}{3}x - 2$.

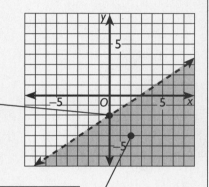

The line shows the ordered pairs for which *y equals* $\frac{2}{3}x - 2$. These ordered pairs are not part of the solution, so the line is dashed.

Test any point in the shaded region, such as $(2, -4)$.

$$2x - 3y > 6$$
$$2(2) - 3(-4) \overset{?}{>} 6$$
$$16 > 6 \text{ Yes.}$$

Graph each inequality.

33. $2x + 4y > 16$

34. $x + 2y \le 9$

35. $-3x + 2y < 6$

36. $5x - 3y \le 15$

37. $2x - 4y > 12$

38. $-3x - 7y \ge -14$

39. $\frac{x}{3} - \frac{y}{2} < 1$

40. $3x - 1.5y > 2$

41. $\frac{3}{2}x - \frac{y}{4} \le 2$

42. $y < -\frac{2}{3}x + 1$

43. $y \ge -x + 5$

44. $y \le 3x - 2$

PRACTICE WORKSHEETS

Instructional Target: Graph systems of inequalities and recognize the solution(s)
from the graph

When graphing systems of inequalities in one or two variables, plot the set of
points that satisfies the conditions of all of the inequalities involved.

Example: Graph the solution set of the system of inequalities.

$$x - 2 > 3$$
$$x \leq 8$$

Solution: Solve each inequality for x, if necessary.

$$x - 2 > 3 \qquad x \leq 8$$
$$x > 5$$

Plot the points that are *both* greater than 5
and less than or equal to 8.

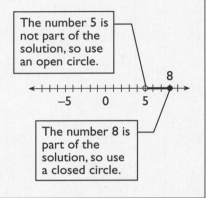

The number 5 is not part of the solution, so use an open circle.

The number 8 is part of the solution, so use a closed circle.

Graph the solution set of each system of inequalities.

45. $x \geq -2$
  $x < 4$

46. $-x < 3$
  $x \leq 5$

47. $x - 4 < 4$
  $x + 1 > 1$

48. $-2x + 3 < 5$
  $4 + x < 7$

49. $-3x - 2 < 4$
  $x \leq 7$

50. $3 - x > 4$
  $x - 2 > -7$

51. $2(x - 3) \leq 3$
  $4 + x > -x - 4$

52. $6 - 2x < 3 + x$
  $2x \leq 7$

53. $5 - (3 - x) < 4$
  $2(x + 3) > 1$

54. $\frac{1}{2}x - 3 < \frac{3}{4}$
  $x + 5 > 5 - x$

55. $(x - 1) - 8 < 3 - x$
  $2 + 2x > -8 - 2x$

56. $\frac{1}{3}x > 2$
  $-\frac{2}{3}x > 4$

Example: Graph the solution set of the system of inequalities.

$$x + y \le 6$$
$$2x - y > -3$$

Then determine whether or not the point (1, 3) is in the solution set.

Solution: Solve each inequality for y, if necessary.

$$x + y \le 6 \qquad\qquad 2x - y > -3$$
$$y \le -x + 6 \qquad\qquad -y > -2x - 3$$
$$\qquad\qquad\qquad\qquad y < 2x + 3$$

Graph the equations $y = -x + 6$ and $y = 2x + 3$.

Shade the region where the points satisfy *both* of the given inequalities.

The shaded region is the solution set. The point (1, 3) is in the solution set.

The line $y = 2x + 3$ is not part of the graph of the solution set, so it is dashed.

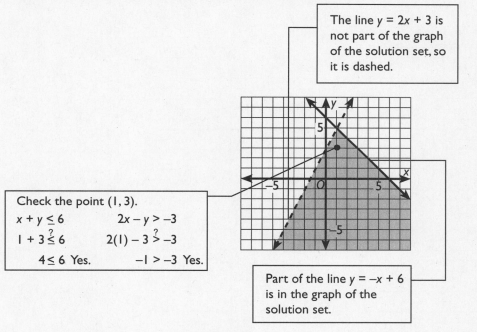

Check the point (1, 3).

$$x + y \le 6 \qquad\qquad 2x - y > -3$$
$$1 + 3 \overset{?}{\le} 6 \qquad\qquad 2(1) - 3 \overset{?}{>} -3$$
$$4 \le 6 \text{ Yes.} \qquad\qquad -1 > -3 \text{ Yes.}$$

Part of the line $y = -x + 6$ is in the graph of the solution set.

Graph the solution set of each system of inequalities.

57. $y < 2x - 3$
$\quad y > -x + 1$

58. $y \ge x + 2$
$\quad y < -2x + 2$

59. $x - 2y \ge 4$
$\quad -2x + y \ge 4$

60. $2x - y < 4$
$\quad 3x + y \le 5$

61. $y < \frac{2}{3}x - 4$
$\quad x \le 6$

62. $y \ge 5x - 3$
$\quad y \le 3$

Determine whether or not the given point is in the solution set of the system of inequalities.

63. $y > -\frac{1}{2}x + 3 \quad$ point: (–2, 4)
$\quad x \le 5$

64. $y > 2x - 4 \quad$ point: (–2, 6)
$\quad y < -x + 5$

65. $2x - y \le 5 \quad$ point: (2, –2)
$\quad -x + 3y < -2$

66. $y > \frac{1}{2}x + 5 \quad$ point: (–2, 7)
$\quad x \le -3$

PRACTICE WORKSHEETS

Cumulative Practice for Objective 2

1. Which graph below best represents the solution to the inequality $x - 3 < 4$?

A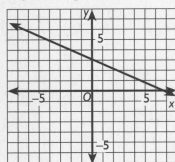
    −5   0   5

B
    −5   0   5

C
    −5   0   5

D
    −5   0   5

E
    −5   0   5

2. Which graph below best represents the equation of a line with a slope of $-\frac{2}{5}$ and a y-intercept of -3?

A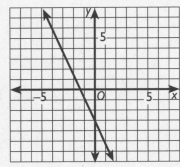

B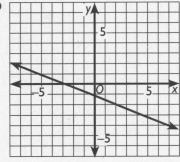

C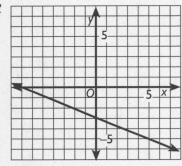

D

E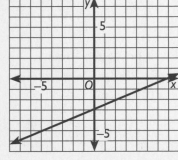

Preparing for the Texas Algebra I End-of-Course Exam

3. The graph of this system of equations is shown at the right.

$$y = -2x + 3$$
$$y = \frac{1}{2}x - 2$$

Which point is in the solution set of the following system of inequalities?

$$y \le -2x + 3$$
$$y < \frac{1}{2}x - 2$$

A (3, 5)
B (3, −5)
C (5, −3)
D (−5, 3)
E (−5, −3)

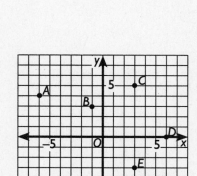

4. Which point lies on the line having as its equation $3x + y = 6$?

A Point A
B Point B
C Point C
D Point D
E Point E

5. Which point does *not* satisfy the inequality $3x - 2y \le 6$?

A (−1, −5)

B $(-2, -\frac{1}{2})$

C (0, −3)

D $(2, \frac{1}{2})$

E (3, 2)

Practice for Objective 3

OBJECTIVE 3 The student will write equations of lines to model problems involving real-world and mathematical situations.

Instructional Target: Write an equation of a line given its graph or description

The slope-intercept form of the equation of a line is $y = mx + b$, where m is the slope and b is the y-intercept.

The slope of the line passing through the points (x_1, y_1) and (x_2, y_2) is given by

$$m = \frac{y_2 - y_1}{x_2 - x_1}.$$

Lines have the same slope if and only if they are parallel.

Example: Write an equation of the line passing through the point $(3, 4)$ with a slope of $-\frac{2}{3}$.

Solution: Use slope-intercept form.

$y = mx + b$	Slope-intercept form
$4 = -\frac{2}{3}(3) + b$	Substitute 3 for x and 4 for y.
$4 = -2 + b$	Simplify.
$6 = b$	Solve for b.

The y-intercept is 6 and the slope is $-\frac{2}{3}$, so the equation in slope-intercept form is $y = -\frac{2}{3} + 6$.

Practice Exercises:

Write an equation for each line described.

1. has slope -2 and y-intercept 4

2. passes through the point $(-3, 5)$ and has slope 3

3. has y-intercept $\frac{4}{3}$ and slope -5

4. passes through the point $(4, 1)$ and has slope $\frac{1}{2}$

5. has slope 4 and y-intercept 7

6. passes through the point $(-8, 5)$ and has slope $\frac{3}{4}$

7. has y-intercept -8 and slope $\frac{5}{7}$

8. passes through the point $(-2, -7)$ and has slope 5

9. passes through $(-1, 2)$ and $(1, 6)$

10. passes through $(6, -2)$ and $(3, -7)$

11. passes through $(5, 2)$ and is parallel to the line $y = -\frac{3}{5}x + 10$

12. passes through $(-6, 4)$ and is parallel to the line $y = \frac{5}{2}x - 1$

Preparing for the Texas Algebra I End-of-Course Exam

Example: Write an equation of the line that is graphed at the right.

Solution: The line crosses the *y*-axis at –3, so the *y*-intercept is –3. To get to another point on the line, move to the right 3 units and up 2 units. Then the slope is $\frac{\text{vertical change}}{\text{horizontal change}} = \frac{2}{3}$.

The slope-intercept form of the equation of the line is

$$y = \frac{2}{3}x - 3.$$

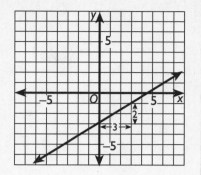

Write an equation for each line.

13.

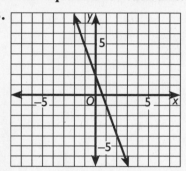

14.

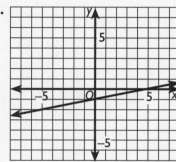

15.

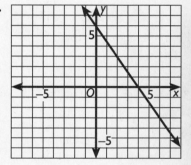

16.

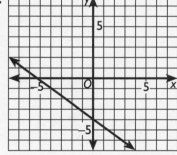

17.

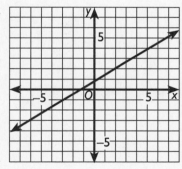

18.

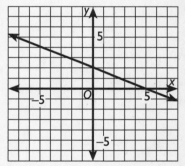

19.

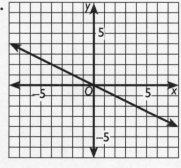

20.

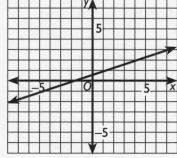

21.

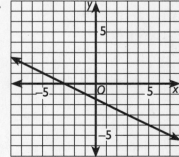

PRACTICE WORKSHEETS

Cumulative Practice for Objective 3

1. The graph of $y = \frac{3}{4}x + 2$ is shown at the right. Which equation best describes a line parallel to the graph of $y = \frac{3}{4}x + 2$?

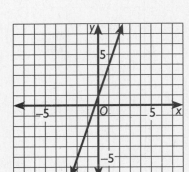

   A $y = -\frac{3}{4}x - 2$

   B $y = \frac{3}{4}x - 2$

   C $y = \frac{4}{3}x + 2$

   D $y = 2(x - \frac{3}{4})$

   E $y = 2(x + \frac{3}{4})$

2. Which equation best describes the graph at the right?

   A $y = x + 3$
   B $y = 3x + 1$
   C $y = -3x + 1$

   D $y = -\frac{1}{3}x + 1$

   E $y = \frac{1}{3}x + 1$

3. Which is an equation for the line passing through $(-1, 4)$ and having a slope of 2?

   A $y = 2x - 9$
   B $y = 2x - 6$
   C $y = 2x - 2$
   D $y = 2x + 2$
   E $y = 2x + 6$

4. Which is an equation for the line passing through $(2, -3)$ and parallel to $y = 3x - 5$?

   A $y = 3x - 9$
   B $y = -3x + 3$

   C $y = \frac{1}{3}x - \frac{11}{3}$

   D $y = -\frac{1}{3}x - \frac{7}{3}$

   E $y = 3x + 3$

Practice for Objective 4

OBJECTIVE 4 **The student will formulate or solve linear equations/inequalities and systems of linear equations that describe real-world and mathematical situations.**

Instructional Target: Formulate or solve linear equations/inequalities

---

Example: George owes Martha $120. He is going to repay her at a rate of $8 per week. Write an equation that gives the amount still to be repaid, r, in terms of the number of weeks, w.

Solution: George is paying Martha at a rate of $8 per week, so the amount he has repaid after w weeks is $8w$. The amount he still owes is found by subtracting the amount he has already repaid from $120.

Amount still to be repaid	= $120 −	Amount already repaid

$$r \quad = \quad 120 - \quad 8w$$

The equation is $r = 120 - 8w$.

Practice Exercises:

Write a linear equation to describe each situation.

1. Amy has $12 to spend on apples and tangerines. Apples cost $.50 per pound and tangerines cost $.75 per pound. Write an equation that gives the relationship between the number of pounds of apples, a, and the number of pounds of tangerines, t, that she can buy.

2. A rectangle is 5 centimeters longer than it is wide. Write an equation that gives the relationship between the perimeter of the rectangle, P, and the width of the rectangle, w.

3. The cost of shipping a package is $3 plus $.80 per pound. Write an equation that gives the cost, c, of shipping the package in terms of the weight of the package in pounds, p.

4. Doug has 3 more dimes than nickels. Write an equation that gives the total amount of money, m, that Doug has in terms of the number of nickels, n, that he has.

5. There were 530 students enrolled at Central High in 1990. The enrollment has been increasing at a rate of 15 students per year since then. Write an equation that gives the number of students enrolled, s, in terms of the number of years, y, since 1990.

6. Fred has a total of $8000 invested in two different accounts. One account earns 6% interest per year and the other earns 5% interest per year. Write an equation that gives the relationship between the total interest, I, earned in one year and the amount, a, invested in the account that earns 6% per year.

PRACTICE WORKSHEETS

7. A bicycle rental shop charges a fee of $5 plus $2 per hour to rent a bicycle. Write an equation to find the total charge, c, for renting a bicycle for h hours.

8. A rectangle has a length of 6 inches. Write an equation to find the area, A, of the rectangle in terms of the width, w, of the rectangle.

9. Herman's Floor Refinishers charges $75 plus $10 per square foot to completely refinish a wood floor. Write an equation that gives the total cost, c, of refinishing a floor in terms of the number of square feet, f.

10. Mary works as a sales assistant in a clothing store. She earns $150 per week plus a 3% commission on the retail cost of everything she sells. Write an equation that gives Mary's total weekly earnings, e, in terms of the total cost, c, of the clothes she sells.

Linear equations in one variable are solved by isolating the variable on one side of the equation. This is done by using the operations of addition, subtraction, multiplication, and division.

Example: Solve for x. $3(4x - 2) = 5x + 4$

Solution:

$$3(4x - 2) = 5x + 4$$

$$12x - 6 = 5x + 4 \qquad \text{Distributive Property}$$

$$12x - 6 - 5x = 5x + 4 - 5x \qquad \text{Subtract } 5x \text{ from both sides.}$$

$$7x - 6 = 4 \qquad \text{Combine like terms.}$$

$$7x - 6 + 6 = 4 + 6 \qquad \text{Add 6 to both sides.}$$

$$7x = 10 \qquad \text{Simplify.}$$

$$\frac{7x}{7} = \frac{10}{7} \qquad \text{Divide both sides by 7.}$$

$$x = \frac{10}{7} \qquad \text{Simplify.}$$

In Exercises 11–22, solve for x.

11. $6x - 4 = 2 - 3x$

12. $3 - 2x = 7 + 4x$

13. $3 + 2x = 4(2 - x)$

14. $2 + 3(x - 1) = 4 + x$

15. $3x = 5 + 2(3 - x) + x$

16. $4 - 2x = 5(1 + x)$

17. $\frac{3}{2}x = 4$

18. $5 - \frac{1}{3}x = x + 1$

19. $6(x - \frac{2}{3}) = 4 - x$

20. $3 - 2(7 - x) = 2x + 4$

21. $6 + 2(3x - 1) = 5 - 2x$

22. $3 - \frac{1}{4}x = x - \frac{1}{2}$

23. Using the information given in Exercise 3, find the number of pounds a package weighs if it costs $13.40 to ship it.

24. Using the information given in Exercise 4, find the number of nickels Doug has if he has $2.55.

25. Using the information given in Exercise 6, find the amount invested at 6% if the interest earned in one year is $450.

26. Using the information given in Exercise 8, find the width of the rectangle if the area is 40 square inches.

PRACTICE WORKSHEETS

Instructional Target: Formulate or solve systems of linear equations

Two or more linear equations in the same variables form a system of linear equations.

Example: The length of a rectangle is 3 centimeters more than twice its width. The perimeter of the rectangle is 96 centimeters. Write a system of equations that will determine the dimensions of the rectangle.

Solution: Use l for the length of the rectangle and w for the width of the rectangle. The first sentence in the example gives the fact that the length is twice the width plus 3 centimeters. The translation into mathematical symbols is $l = 2w + 3$. The second sentence gives the perimeter as 96 centimeters. The perimeter of a rectangle is found by adding twice the length and twice the width. The mathematical statement is $2l + 2w = 96$. The system of equations is:

$$l = 2w + 3$$
$$2l + 2w = 96$$

Write a system of linear equations to describe each situation.

27. The sum of two numbers is 20. The difference of the two numbers is twice the smaller number. Write a system of equations that will determine the two numbers.

28. Three apples and 2 peaches sell for $1.25. Five apples and 1 peach sell for $1.50. Write a system of equations that will determine the cost of an apple.

29. Jack bought 7 tickets for a movie. He paid $7 for each adult ticket and $4 for each child ticket. Jack spent $40 for the tickets. Write a system of equations that will determine how many adult tickets Jack bought.

30. Fran invested a total of $8000 in two mutual funds. One fund paid 12% interest for the year and the other fund paid 9% interest for the year. Altogether Fran received $810 in interest for the year. Write a system of equations that will determine how much Fran invested in each fund.

31. A pizza chef made and sold a total of 100 pizzas that were either cheese or pepperoni. The cheese pizzas sold for $9 each and the pepperoni pizzas sold for $11 each. If the total receipts were $1026, write a system of equations that will determine how many cheese pizzas were sold.

32. Three sandwiches were given to each adult and two sandwiches were given to each child who went on the Jefferson Middle School annual outing. There were 40 people on the bus and a total of 89 sandwiches were given out. Write a system of equations that will determine how many adults and how many children were on the trip.

PRACTICE WORKSHEETS

Example: The equations of two lines are $x - 2y = -1$ and $2x - 3y = 4$. Find the point where the two lines intersect.

Solution: To find the point of intersection, solve the system.

$$x - 2y = -1$$
$$2x - 3y = 4$$

That is, find a pair of numbers, x and y, that makes both equations true. There are two commonly used methods for solving systems of linear equations. Each is shown below.

Method 1: Substitution

Step 1:
Solve the first equation for x.

$$x - 2y = -1$$
$x - 2y + 2y = -1 + 2y$ Add $2y$ to both sides.
$\quad\quad x = -1 + 2y$ Simplify.

Step 2:
Substitute this expression for x in the second equation and solve for y.

$$2x - 3y = 4$$
$2(-1 + 2y) - 3y = 4$ Substitute $-1 + 2y$ for x.
$-2 + 4y - 3y = 4$ Multiply.
$-2 + y = 4$ Combine like terms.
$-2 + y + 2 = 4 + 2$ Add 2 to both sides.
$y = 6$ Simplify.

Step 3:
Find x using the value of y from Step 2.
From Step 1, $x = -1 + 2y$.
$x = -1 + 2(6)$ Substitute the value of y.
$x = 11$ Simplify.
The point of intersection is (11, 6).

Method 2: Elimination

Step 1:
Multiply the first equation by -2 so that the x-terms have opposite coefficients.
$x - 2y = -1$
$-2(x - 2y) = -2(-1)$ Multiply both sides by -2.
$-2x + 4y = 2$ Simplify.

Step 2:
Add this new equation to the second equation and solve for y.
$-2x + 4y = 2$ New equation
$\underline{2x - 3y = 4}$ Second equation
$y = 6$ Add the equations.

Step 3:
Find x using the value of y from Step 2.
$x - 2y = -1$ Original first equation
$x - 2(6) = -1$ Substitute the value of y.
$x = 11$ Solve for x.

The point of intersection is (11, 6).

Solve each system.

33. $x + y = 7$
$2x - y = 2$

34. $y = 3x - 1$
$2x - y = 2$

35. $x - 3y = 7$
$5x + y = 3$

36. $2x + y = 7$
$x - 2y = -4$

37. $x = 4 - y$
$3x + 2y = 11$

38. $y = x + 6$
$x + y = -6$

39. $4x - 3y = 1$
$2x + 6y = 3$

40. $3x - y = -1$
$y = 6x$

41. $2y = 4x + 8$
$x - 3y = -7$

42. $4x - 3y = 9$
$y = 8x - 8$

43. $x + 5y = 3$
$4x + 7y = -1$

44. $2x - 5y = 14$
$4x = 3y + 7$

Preparing for the Texas Algebra I End-of-Course Exam

Cumulative Practice for Objective 4

1. Springfield Public Pool must have one lifeguard for every 12 swimmers, plus a pool manager, a cashier, and a nurse on staff. Which equation below shows the relationship between the number of swimmers, s, and the number of staff people, p, required?

A $p = 3 + \frac{s}{12}$

B $s = 3 + \frac{p}{12}$

C $p = 3s + 12$

D $p = 3 + 12s$

E $p = 15s$

2. Mr. Kaplan bought 11 tickets to the circus and spent $50. He bought child tickets for $4 each and he bought adult tickets for $7 each. Which system of equations will determine the number of adult tickets, a, and the number of child tickets, c, he bought?

A $7a + 7c = 50$
     $a + c = 11$

B $a + c = 11$
     $7c + 4a = 50$

C $a + c = 50$
     $a + c = 11$

D $a + c = 11$
     $7a + 4c = 50$

E $a - 11 = c$
     $11ac = 50$

3. A rectangle is 6 inches longer than it is wide. Which equation gives the relationship between the perimeter, p, of the rectangle and the width of the rectangle, w?

A $p = 2w + 6$

B $p = 4w + 12$

C $p = 2w - 6$

D $p = 4(w + 6)$

E $p = 12w$

4. What is the solution to the equation $3(2x - 4) = 4x + 8$?

A -2

B 6

C 10

D 15

E 20

PRACTICE WORKSHEETS

5. Two lines have equations given by the system shown below.

$$3x + y = 6$$
$$4y = 3x - 21$$

What is the point of intersection of the two lines?

A $(5, -9)$

B $(\frac{1}{3}, 5)$

C $(\frac{1}{3}, -5)$

D $(-5, -9)$

E $(3, -3)$

6. There were 24 people in the school play. There were three times as many students in the play as teachers. Which system of equations could be used to find the number of teachers, t, and the number of students, s, in the play?

A $s + t = 24$
      $s = t + 3$

B $s - 24 = t$
      $s = t + 3$

C $ts = 24$
      $s = 3t$

D $t + s = 24$
      $t = 3s$

E $t + s = 24$
      $s = 3t$

7. Carrie has 26 coins, all nickels and dimes, amounting to $2.20. A system of equations describing this situation is shown below and can be solved for d and n.

$$n + d = 26$$
$$5n + 10d = 220$$

How many nickels does Carrie have?

A 6
B 8
C 10
D 12
E 14

Practice for Objective 5

OBJECTIVE 5 The student will formulate or solve absolute value equations/inequalities and quadratic equations that describe real-world and mathematical situations.

Instructional Target: Solve absolute value equations/inequalities (optional)

The expression inside the absolute value symbol, $|\ \ |$, may be either positive or negative. If $|A| = B$, where B is positive, then $A = B$ or $A = -B$. However, the equation $|A| = B$ has no solution if B is negative.

Example: Solve for x. $|x + 3| = 5$

Solution: The expression inside the absolute value symbol, $x + 3$, could be equal to 5 or -5, so

$$x + 3 = 5 \text{ or } x + 3 = -5$$
$$x = 2 \text{ or } \qquad x = -8$$

Check the results. $|2 + 3| = 5 \checkmark \qquad |-8 + 3| = 5 \checkmark$

Practice Exercises:

Solve for x in each of the following equations.

1. $|x - 3| = 7$

2. $|x + 4| = 13$

3. $|x - 1| = 3$

4. $|x - 9| = -2$

5. $|2x + 4| = 12$

6. $|3x - 1| = 8$

7. $|5x + 7| = 17$

8. $|4 - x| = 5$

9. $|7 - 2x| = 11$

10. $|6x + 1| = 13$

11. $|4x - 2| = 18$

12. $|x| - 4 = 8$

13. $|3x| - 5 = 4$

14. $3 - |x| = 1$

15. $2 + |x - 3| = 7$

16. $|2x - 1| - 3 = 10$

If $|A| > B$, where B is positive, then $A < -B$ or $A > B$.

If $|A| < B$, where B is positive, then $A > -B$ and $A < B$.

Example: Solve for x in each inequality.

      a. $|2x - 3| > 7$ **b.** $|x + 4| \le 9$

Solution: **a.** $2x - 3 < -7$ or $2x - 3 > 7$ **b.** $x + 4 \ge -9$ and $x + 4 \le 9$

              $2x < -4 \qquad 2x > 10$ $x \ge -13 \qquad x \le 5$

              $x < -2 \qquad x > 5$

      The solution is $x < -2$ or $x > 5$.   The solution is $x \ge -13$ and $x \le 5$ or simply $-13 \le x \le 5$.

Solve for *x* in each inequality.

17. $|x| \leq 5$

18. $|x| > 2$

19. $|x| \geq 4$

20. $|x| < 1$

21. $|x + 2| \geq 3$

22. $|x - 1| < 8$

23. $|x + 4| > 9$

24. $|x - 3| \leq 2$

25. $|x + 5| \geq 7$

26. $|2x - 1| < 7$

27. $|x - 2| \leq 18$

28. $|3x + 1| \leq 8$

29. $|3x| - 4 \geq 5$

30. $|2 - x| > 5$

31. $|2x - 3| \geq 7$

32. $|x - 1| < 10$

Instructional Target: Formulate or solve quadratic equations

Functions that have as their rule an equation in the form $y = ax^2 + bx + c$ are called **quadratic functions**. Equations of the form $ax^2 + bx + c = 0$ are called **quadratic equations**. The solution of the quadratic equation $ax^2 + bx + c = 0$ is given by the **quadratic formula** shown below.

$$x = \frac{-b + \sqrt{b^2 - 4ac}}{2a} \text{ or } x = \frac{-b - \sqrt{b^2 - 4ac}}{2a}$$

Example: Solve each equation for *x*.

        a. $3x^2 + 2x - 1 = 0$

        b. $2x^2 = x + 5$

Solution: **a.** In $3x^2 + 2x - 1 = 0$, $a = 3$, $b = 2$, and $c = -1$.

The solution is:

$$x = \frac{-2 \pm \sqrt{2^2 - 4(3)(-1)}}{2(3)}$$

$$= \frac{-2 \pm \sqrt{16}}{6}$$

$$= \frac{-2 \pm 4}{6}$$

$$= \frac{-2 - 4}{6} \text{ or } \frac{-2 + 4}{6}$$

$$x = -1 \text{ or } \frac{1}{3}$$

b. First write $2x^2 = x + 5$ in $ax^2 + bx + c = 0$ form. You get $2x^2 - x - 5 = 0$, so that $a = 2$, $b = -1$, and $c = -5$

The solution is:

$$x = \frac{-(-1) \pm \sqrt{(-1)^2 - 4(2)(-5)}}{2(2)}$$

$$= \frac{1 \pm \sqrt{41}}{4}$$

$$x = \frac{1 - \sqrt{41}}{4} \text{ or } \frac{1 + \sqrt{41}}{4}$$

$$x \approx -1.351 \text{ or } 1.851$$

PRACTICE
WORKSHEETS

Solve each equation for x.

33. $x^2 - 4x - 5 = 0$ **34.** $x^2 + 2x - 8 = 0$ **35.** $x^2 = 7x + 30$

36. $2x^2 - 3x = 5$ **37.** $3x^2 + 2x = 5$ **38.** $3x^2 - x - 2 = 0$

39. $x^2 - x - 4 = 0$ **40.** $5x^2 = x + 1$ **41.** $x^2 - x + 4 = 0$

42. $2x^2 + x = 6$ **43.** $6x^2 - x - 2 = 0$ **44.** $5x^2 - 2x - 2 = 0$

45. $-2x^2 + 3x + 1 = 0$ **46.** $-x^2 - 3x - 5 = 0$ **47.** $6x + 1 = 3x^2$

Example: The area of the rectangle shown is 24 square inches. Write an equation that could be used to find the width, w, of the rectangle.

Solution: The area of a rectangle is $A = $ (length)(width).
$24 = (2w + 3)(w)$
$24 = 2w^2 + 3w$
The equation is $2w^2 + 3w - 24 = 0$.

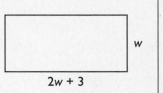

Write a quadratic equation to describe each situation.

48. Two squares are shown. Write an equation to find the length of a side of the smaller square if the difference between their areas is 25 square centimeters.

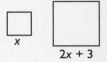

49. A rectangular swimming pool is 4 meters longer than it is wide. Write an equation that will determine the dimensions of the pool if its area is 96 square meters.

50. The sum of the squares of two consecutive integers is 113. Write an equation that will determine the two integers.

51. The area of the triangle shown is 84 square feet. Write an equation that can be used to determine the lengths of the sides of the triangle. (The triangle at the right is not drawn with its actual shape.)

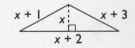

52. Frank bought $2x + 1$ tickets to a show. Each ticket cost $x - 1$ dollars. Write an equation that will determine T, the total amount Frank paid for the tickets.

53. Julie drove at a rate of $2x - 3$ miles per hour for $x + 1$ hours. Write an equation that will determine d, the total distance that Julie drove.

54. A cattle rancher has 120 feet of fencing to form a cattle corral. She plans to use a stone wall for one side of the corral. If she uses x feet of fencing for the sides perpendicular to the stone wall and she wants to enclose 1800 square feet of ground, write an equation that will determine how much fencing to use for each side of the corral.

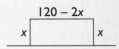

Preparing for the Texas Algebra I End-of-Course Exam
83

Cumulative Practice for Objective 5

1. What are the solutions to the equation $|2x| - 8 = 20$? (optional)

 A $x = -14$ or $x = 14$
 B $x = 12$ or $x = 28$
 C $x = -12$ or $x = 12$
 D $x = 6$ or $x = 14$
 E $x = -6$ or $x = 6$

2. In order for a certain house plant to survive, the temperature must remain close to 75° Fahrenheit. The acceptable range of temperatures is given by $|T - 75| \leq 8$. What is the acceptable range of temperatures for the plant? (optional)

 A $T < 67°$ or $T > 83°$
 B $T \leq 67°$ or $T \geq 83°$
 C $67° \leq T \leq 83°$
 D $T > 67°$
 E $T \leq 83°$

3. What is the solution to the equation $x^2 - 2x - 1 = 7$?

 A $x = -1$ or $x = 8$
 B $x = -1$ or $x = 7$
 C $x = -8$ or $x = 1$
 D $x = -2$ or $x = 4$
 E $x = -4$ or $x = 2$

4. The length of a rectangle is 5 inches more than twice its width, x. The area of the rectangle is 150 square inches. Which equation below can be used to determine the dimensions of the rectangle?

 A $2x + 5 = 150$
 B $6x + 10 = 150$
 C $2x^2 + 5 = 150$
 D $2x^2 + 5x + 150 = 0$
 E $2x^2 + 5x - 150 = 0$

5. What is the solution to the equation $|3x - 9| = 15$? (optional)

 A $x = -2$ or $x = 3$
 B $x = -2$ or $x = 8$
 C $x = -2$ or $x = 15$
 D $x = 3$ or $x = 8$
 E $x = 5$ or $x = 8$

Practice for Objective 6

OBJECTIVE 6 The student will perform operations on and factor polynomials that describe real-world and mathematical situations.

Instructional Target: Perform operations on polynomials

A **monomial** is a numeral, a variable, or an indicated product of a numeral and one or more variables. The expressions -6 and $4x^2$ are monomials. A **polynomial** is a monomial or a sum of monomials. The algebraic expression $3x^2y + (-2x^4)$, or $3x^2y - 2x^4$ is a polynomial. Its **coefficients** are 3 and -2.

To add or subtract polynomials, combine like terms.

Example: Perform the indicated operations and simplify.

    a. $(x^3 + 3x^2 + 2) + (2x^3 - 4x + 4)$

    b. $(3x^4 - 2x^2 + 3) - (x^4 - 2x^3 + x^2)$

Solution: **a.** x^3 and $2x^3$ are like terms. Their sum is $3x^3$.

        2 and 4 are like terms. Their sum is 6.

        $3x^2$ and $-4x$ cannot be combined with any terms.

        Therefore, $(x^3 + 3x^2 + 2) + (2x^3 - 4x + 4) = 3x^3 + 3x^2 - 4x + 6$.

    b. Add the opposites of the terms of the polynomial that is being subtracted.

        $(3x^4 - 2x^2 + 3) - (x^4 - 2x^3 + x^2)$ becomes $(3x^4 - 2x^2 + 3) + (-x^4 + 2x^3 - x^2)$.

        Now add like terms: $3x^4$ and $-x^4$ are like terms. Their sum is $2x^4$.

                $-2x^2$ and $-x^2$ are like terms. Their sum is $-3x^2$.

                3 and $2x^3$ cannot be combined with any terms.

        Therefore, $(3x^4 - 2x^2 + 3) - (x^4 - 2x^3 + x^2) = 2x^4 + 2x^3 - 3x^2 + 3$.

Practice Exercises:

Perform the indicated operations and simplify.

1. $(6x^4 - 7x^3 - 5) + (x^4 + 3x^2 - 2x - 8)$

2. $(4t^2 + 7t) - (t^2 - 8t + 2)$

3. $(9n^2 + 5n) + (n^2 + 6n + 12)$

4. $(5x^3 - 7x^2 + 12) - (4x^3 - 5x^2 + 6x)$

5. $(6a^2 - 2a - 7) + (4a^2 + 2a - 4)$

6. $(5x - 3) + (6x - 4) - (-3x + 6)$

7. $(5x^5 - 4x^4 + 23) - (-5x^5 - 4x^4 - 23)$

8. $(7t^3 - 2t^2 - 12) + (8t^3 - 2t + 12)$

9. $(5ab - 7b + 9a) + (3a - 2b + 4ab)$

10. $(3x - 2xy + 5y) - (6x + 4y - 3xy)$

11. $(4y^2 - 8y - 4) + (6y^3 + 8y + 4)$

12. $(4x^2 - 3xy + y) - (4y^2 + 6x^2 - 2xy)$

To multiply two polynomials, multiply each term in the first polynomial by each term in the second polynomial and combine like terms.

Example: Multiply. $(3x^2 - 4x + 2)(6x - 5)$

Solution: Each term of the first polynomial must be multiplied by each term of the second polynomial.

$$(3x^2)(6x) + (3x^2)(-5) + (-4x)(6x) + (-4x)(-5) + (2)(6x) + (2)(-5)$$

Multiply the factors.

$$18x^3 + (-15x^2) + (-24x^2) + 20x + 12x + (-10)$$

Add like terms.

$-15x^2$ and $-24x^2$ are like terms. Their sum is $-39x^2$.

$20x$ and $12x$ are like terms. Their sum is $32x$.

$18x^3$ and -10 cannot be combined with any terms.

Therefore, the product is $18x^3 - 39x^2 + 32x - 10$.

In Exercises 13–24, multiply and simplify.

13. $(x - 5)(x + 3)$

14. $(t^2 + 7t)(t + 2)$

15. $(n + 5)(n^2 - n + 2)$

16. $(5x + 12)(x^2 - x + 6)$

17. $(a^2 - 2a + 5)(2a - 3)$

18. $(5x - 3)(6x - 5)$

19. $(5x - 4)(x^2 - 4x - 2)$

20. $(t^2 + 2)(t^3 - 2)$

21. $(5a - 7)(3a + 4)$

22. $(3x + 5)(6x + 4)$

23. $(4y^2 - 8y - 4)(y + 4)$

24. $(4x - 3)(6x - 2)$

25. Find the perimeter of a rectangle that has length $3x + 6$ and width $5x + 2$.

26. Find the perimeter of a rectangle that has length $2x^2 - 3x + 1$ and width $5x - 4$.

27. Find the perimeter of a rectangle that has length $3x + xy + 2y$ and width $6x - 4y$.

28. Find the area of a rectangle that has length $2x + 1$ and width $3x + 4$.

29. Find the area of a rectangle that has length $3x - 2$ and width $x + y$.

30. Find the area of a rectangle that has length $x^2 + 4x$ and width $5x + 6$.

PRACTICE WORKSHEETS

Instructional Target: Factor polynomials using models

Example: Factor the polynomial $x^2 + 3x + 2$ by using algebra tiles.

  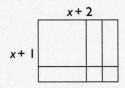

Key: $= x^2$ $= x$ $\square = 1$

Solution: The area of the rectangle is $x^2 + 3x + 2$. The length of the rectangle is $x + 2$ and the width of the rectangle is $x + 1$ as shown below.

$x + 2$

$x + 1$

The area of a rectangle is (length) times (width), so the factorization of $x^2 + 3x + 2$ is $(x + 2)(x + 1)$.

Use the model to factor each polynomial.

31. $x^2 + 5x + 6$ **32.** $x^2 + 5x + 4$ **33.** $x^2 + 6x + 8$

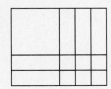   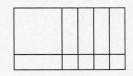   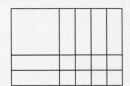

34. $2x^2 + 5x + 2$ **35.** $2x^2 + 5x + 3$ **36.** $2x^2 + 7x + 3$

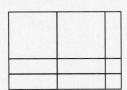   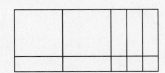   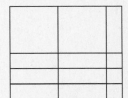

37. $3x^2 + 8x + 4$ **38.** $3x^2 + 5x + 2$

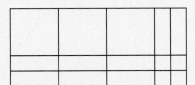   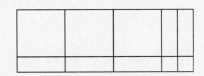

PRACTICE WORKSHEETS

> **Example:** Factor each of the following.
>
>   **a.** $3x^3 - 6x^2 + 12x$
>
>   **b.** $x^2 - 5x - 6$
>
> **Solution:** **a.** All three terms have the common factor $3x$, so the factored form is
> $3x(x^2 - 2x + 4)$. The quadratic polynomial $x^2 - 2x + 4$ does not factor.
>
>   **b.** If the polynomial is to have an x-term after the factors are multiplied together,
>   then the factors of x^2 must be x and x. The possible pairs of integer factors of
> -6 are: 1 and -6, -1 and 6, 2 and -3, and -2 and 3. If $x^2 - 5x - 6$ can be
>   factored at all, then the factorization must be one of the following.
>
> $$(x + 2)(x - 3)$$
> $$(x - 2)(x + 3)$$
> $$(x + 1)(x - 6)$$
> $$(x - 1)(x + 6)$$
>
> Multiply out each indicated product.
>
> $$(x + 2)(x - 3) = x^2 - x - 6$$
> $$(x - 2)(x + 3) = x^2 + x - 6$$
> $$(x + 1)(x - 6) = x^2 - 5x - 6 \longleftarrow \text{This is the original polynomial.}$$
> $$(x - 1)(x + 6) = x^2 + 5x - 6$$
>
> The factorization is $(x + 1)(x - 6)$.

Factor each polynomial.

39. $x^2 + 4x$ **40.** $4x^3 - 6x$

41. $4x^3 - 8x^2$ **42.** $4y^3 - 6y^2 + 14y$

43. $6t^4 - 12t^3 + 18t^2$ **44.** $12b^3 + 15b^2 - 9b$

45. $x^2 - 4x - 21$ **46.** $y^2 + 5y + 6$

47. $t^2 + 7t - 8$ **48.** $x^2 - 2x - 8$

49. $2x^2 + x - 1$ **50.** $2x^2 + 11x + 15$

51. $3y^2 + 8y - 3$ **52.** $4t^2 + t - 3$

53. $2x^2 - 3x - 20$ **54.** $2x^2 + 2x - 12$

55. $3y^2 - 6y - 24$ **56.** $8t^2 - 4t - 12$

57. $x^2 - 4$ **58.** $x^2 + 6x + 9$

Cumulative Practice for Objective 6

1. The sides of a triangle have lengths $x^2 + 1$, $2x - 3$, and $2x^2 + x$. Which of the following gives the perimeter of the triangle?

  A $2x^2 + 2x - 2$
  B $3x^2 + 3x + 4$
  C $3x^2 + 3x - 2$
  D $x^2 + x - 2$
  E $2x^4 + 2x^2 - 3$

2. The two legs of a right triangle have lengths $2x + 6$ and $3x + 1$. Which of the following gives the area of the triangle?

  A $5x + 7$
  B $10x + 14$
  C $6x^2 + 7$
  D $6x^2 + 20x + 6$
  E $3x^2 + 10x + 3$

3. The polynomial $4x^2 + 8x + 3$ is modeled at the right using algebra tiles. Which of the following are the factors of this polynomial?

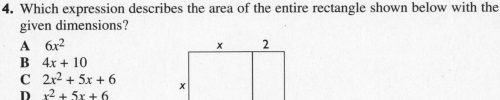

  A $(2x - 1)(2x - 3)$
  B $(2x + 1)(2x + 3)$
  C $(4x + 1)(x + 3)$
  D $(2x - 1)(2x + 3)$
  E $(2x - 3)(2x + 1)$

4. Which expression describes the area of the entire rectangle shown below with the given dimensions?

  A $6x^2$
  B $4x + 10$
  C $2x^2 + 5x + 6$
  D $x^2 + 5x + 6$
  E $x^2 + x + 6$

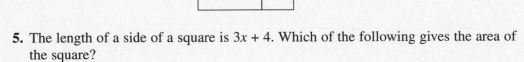

5. The length of a side of a square is $3x + 4$. Which of the following gives the area of the square?

  A $9x^2 - 16$
  B $9x^2 + 12x + 16$
  C $6x + 8$
  D $12x + 16$
  E $9x^2 + 24x + 16$

Practice for Objective 7

| OBJECTIVE 7 | The student will solve rational and radical equations that describe real-world and mathematical situations. (This objective is optional.) |

Instructional Target: Solve rational equations

A **rational equation** is an equation that contains at least one expression that is written in fraction form. One way to solve such equations is to eliminate the denominators by multiplying every term by the least common multiple of the denominators.

Example: Solve for y. $\frac{y}{2} + \frac{1}{4} = \frac{y}{6}$

Solution: The least common multiple of the denominators is 12. Multiply each term by 12 and solve the resulting equation.

$12(\frac{y}{2}) + 12(\frac{1}{4}) = 12(\frac{y}{6})$ Multiply each term by 12.

$6y + 3 = 2y$ Simplify.

$6y + 3 - 2y = 2y - 2y$ Subtract 2y from both sides.

$4y + 3 = 0$ Simplify.

$4y + 3 - 3 = 0 - 3$ Subtract 3 from both sides.

$4y = -3$ Simplify.

$y = -\frac{3}{4}$ Divide both sides by 4.

Check the result in the original equation. $\frac{-\frac{3}{4}}{2} + \frac{1}{4} \overset{?}{=} \frac{-\frac{3}{4}}{6}$

$-\frac{3}{8} + \frac{1}{4} \overset{?}{=} -\frac{3}{24}$

$-\frac{3}{8} + \frac{2}{8} \overset{?}{=} -\frac{1}{8}$

$-\frac{1}{8} = -\frac{1}{8} ✓$

Practice Exercises:

Solve each equation for x.

1. $\frac{2x}{7} - \frac{3x}{2} = \frac{1}{3}$

2. $\frac{3x}{2} + \frac{8 - 4x}{7} = 3$

3. $\frac{x + 1}{4} - \frac{3}{2} = \frac{2x - 9}{10}$

4. $\frac{x}{4} - \frac{1}{3} = \frac{x}{2}$

5. $\frac{x}{7} + \frac{x + 1}{4} = 6$

6. $\frac{x}{4} - \frac{x + 6}{5} = 1$

7. $\frac{2x}{3} + \frac{x}{6} = \frac{5}{3}$

8. $\frac{x - 2}{5} - \frac{x + 1}{4} = x - 8$

9. $\frac{3}{4} - \frac{x + 3}{6} = \frac{x}{12}$

10. $\frac{3x}{5} - \frac{x}{10} = 1$

11. $\frac{x}{3} = \frac{x + 1}{4} - \frac{1}{12}$

12. $\frac{2x - 1}{7} + \frac{x}{8} = \frac{3}{2}$

If the denominators contain a variable, then the least common multiple of the denominators will include that variable.

Example: Solve for x. $\dfrac{9}{2x} + \dfrac{3}{x} = \dfrac{8}{x} - \dfrac{1}{16}$

Solution: The least common multiple of the denominators is $16x$.

$$16x\left(\tfrac{9}{2x}\right) + 16x\left(\tfrac{3}{x}\right) = 16x\left(\tfrac{8}{x}\right) - 16x\left(\tfrac{1}{16}\right) \qquad \text{Multiply each term by } 16x.$$

$$72 + 48 = 128 - x \qquad \text{Simplify.}$$

$$120 = 128 - x \qquad \text{Add.}$$

$$120 - 128 = 128 - x - 128 \qquad \text{Subtract 128 from both sides.}$$

$$-8 = -x \qquad \text{Simplify.}$$

$$8 = x \qquad \text{Divide both sides by } -1.$$

Check the solution. When a variable is in the denominator, check that no solution for the equation makes any denominator equal to zero. Substitute $x = 8$ in the original equation.

$$\dfrac{9}{2(8)} + \dfrac{3}{8} \stackrel{?}{=} \dfrac{8}{8} - \dfrac{1}{16}$$

$$\dfrac{9}{16} + \dfrac{6}{16} \stackrel{?}{=} \dfrac{16}{16} - \dfrac{1}{16}$$

$$\dfrac{15}{16} = \dfrac{15}{16} \quad \checkmark$$

In Exercises 13–21, solve for x in each equation.

13. $\dfrac{x-2}{x} = \dfrac{14}{3x} - \dfrac{1}{3}$

14. $\dfrac{x-4}{x} = \dfrac{16}{5x} - \dfrac{1}{5}$

15. $\dfrac{1+x}{x} - \dfrac{3}{x} = 0$

16. $\dfrac{12}{x} + \dfrac{1}{4x} = 7$

17. $\dfrac{5}{x} - \dfrac{x-2}{x} = \dfrac{3}{4}$

18. $\dfrac{3}{2x} = \dfrac{6}{x+6}$

19. $\dfrac{4}{x-2} = \dfrac{2}{x-3}$

20. $3 - \dfrac{5}{3x} = 2 + \dfrac{1}{3x}$

21. $\dfrac{2}{x+3} + \dfrac{1}{2} = \dfrac{x+7}{2x+6}$

22. The perimeter of a rectangle is 10. The length of the rectangle is $\dfrac{6}{x}$ and the width is $\dfrac{4}{x}$. Find the dimensions of the rectangle.

23. The perimeter of a triangle is $\dfrac{27}{2}$. The sides have lengths of $\dfrac{13}{y}, \dfrac{20}{y}$, and $\dfrac{15}{2y}$. Find the actual lengths of the sides of the triangle.

Instructional Target: Solve radical equations

An equation that contains a variable expression under a square root sign is an example of a **radical equation**. To solve an equation of this type, transform the equation so that the square root expression is alone on one side of the equal sign. Then square both sides of the equation.

Example: Solve for x. $\sqrt{x} + 4 = 7$

Solution: Get the radical expression alone on one side of the equation, square both sides of the equation, and solve the resulting equation.

$$\sqrt{x} + 4 - 4 = 7 - 4 \qquad \text{Subtract 4 from both sides.}$$
$$\sqrt{x} = 3 \qquad \text{Simplify.}$$
$$(\sqrt{x})^2 = (3)^2 \qquad \text{Square both sides.}$$
$$x = 9 \qquad \text{Simplify.}$$

Always check the answer of a radical equation. Substitute $x = 9$ in the original equation.

$$\sqrt{9} + 4 \stackrel{?}{=} 7$$
$$3 + 4 \stackrel{?}{=} 7$$
$$7 = 7 \quad \checkmark$$

In Exercises 24–35, solve for x. Check your answers.

24. $\sqrt{x - 3} = 5$

25. $\sqrt{x - 2} - 6 = 0$

26. $\sqrt{4x - 3} = 3$

27. $\sqrt{1 - 3x} - 10 = -3$

28. $3\sqrt{x} + 2 = 8$

29. $\sqrt{x} - 4 = -12$

30. $\sqrt{x + 1} - 6 = 2$

31. $\sqrt{3x} + 4 = 7$

32. $\sqrt{x} - 3 = 0$

33. $4\sqrt{x} = 20$

34. $3\sqrt{x - 2} - 5 = 1$

35. $\sqrt{x + 2} + 3 = 1$

36. An equilateral triangle has sides of length $\sqrt{x + 1}$ units. If the perimeter is 12 units, find the value of x.

37. A rectangle has an area of 16 square units. The length of the rectangle is 8 units and the width is $\sqrt{2x + 1}$ units. Find the value of x.

38. A square with sides of length $\sqrt{3x + 1}$ units has a perimeter of 20 units. Find the value of x.

Preparing for the Texas Algebra I End-of-Course Exam
Copyright © McDougal Littell Inc. All rights reserved.

Cumulative Practice for Objective 7

1. Find the value of x in the equation $\frac{2}{3} - \frac{4}{x} = \frac{4}{3x}$.

A -4

B $-\frac{6}{5}$

C $-\frac{1}{2}$

D 4

E 8

2. Find the value of x in the equation $4\sqrt{x} - 5 = 4$.

A $\frac{1}{16}$

B 1

C $\frac{3}{2}$

D $\frac{9}{4}$

E $\frac{81}{16}$

3. Find the value of x in the equation $\frac{2x-1}{x+2} = \frac{5}{3}$.

A $\frac{5}{11}$

B 1

C $\frac{11}{7}$

D 3

E 13

4. Find the value of x in the equation $\sqrt{2x+1} + 3 = 7$.

A $\frac{3}{2}$

B 4

C $\frac{15}{2}$

D 16

E $\frac{99}{2}$

5. A rectangle with an area of 12 square units has a width of $\frac{3}{2}$ units and a length of $\sqrt{2x+3}$ units. Find the value of x.

A $\frac{5}{2}$

B $\frac{15}{2}$

C $\frac{61}{2}$

D $\frac{67}{2}$

E $\frac{321}{2}$

Preparing for the Texas Algebra I End-of-Course Exam

PRACTICE WORKSHEETS

Practice for Objective 8

PRACTICE WORKSHEETS

OBJECTIVE 8 The student will use problem-solving strategies to analyze, solve, and/or justify solutions to real-world and mathematical problems involving exponents, quadratic situations, or right triangles.

Instructional Target: Analyze and/or solve problems involving the laws of exponents

In the expression b^a ("b to the ath power" or "b to the power a"), b is called the **base** and a is the **exponent**. Two or more expressions that have the same base can be combined with the aid of the following laws of exponents.

Law 1: $b^a \cdot b^c = b^{a+c}$ Law 2: $\dfrac{b^a}{b^c} = b^{a-c}$

Three other commonly used laws of exponents are the following.

Law 3: $(b^a)^c = b^{ac}$ Law 4: $b^0 = 1$ Law 5: $b^{-a} = \dfrac{1}{b^a}$

Example: Simplify each of the following.

    a. $\dfrac{x^2 \cdot x^6}{x^4}$ **b.** $(2^2)^3 + 2 \cdot 3^{-1} - 4^0$

Solution: **a.** $\dfrac{x^2 \cdot x^6}{x^4}$ **b.** $(2^2)^3 + 2 \cdot 3^{-1} - 4^0$

         $= \dfrac{x^{2+6}}{x^4}$ Use law 1 above. $= 2^{2 \cdot 3} + 2 \cdot 3^{-1} - 4^0$ Use law 3.

         $= \dfrac{x^8}{x^4}$ Simplify. $= 2^6 + 2 \cdot \dfrac{1}{3} - 4^0$ Simplify and use law 5.

         $= x^{8-4}$ Use law 2. $= 64 + \dfrac{2}{3} - 1$ Simplify and use law 4.

         $= x^4$ Simplify. $= \dfrac{191}{3}$ Combine terms.

Practice Exercises:

Simplify.

1. $x^2 \cdot x^5 \cdot x^3$ **2.** $\dfrac{a^8}{a^2}$ **3.** $c^3 \cdot c^2 \cdot b^4$ **4.** $5 \cdot 6^0 + \dfrac{3 \cdot 2^6}{2^4}$ **5.** $(y^2)^{-4}(y^4)^2$

6. $3 \cdot 2^2 - 2 \cdot 3^3$ **7.** $(x^2)^{-3}$ **8.** $\dfrac{x^2 y^4}{x^3 y^2}$ **9.** $(a^2 b^3)^3$ **10.** $\dfrac{(x^0 y^4)^2}{x^{-3} y^3}$

Give the value of each.

11. $2 - 3 \cdot 2^x$ if $x = 3$ **12.** $3 \cdot b^a$ if $b = -2$ and $a = 3$ **13.** $5 \cdot 3^t$ if $t = -2$

A number is expressed in scientific notation if it is written in the form $a \times 10^x$, where $1 \le a < 10$ and x is an integer.

Example: **a.** Earth is approximately 92,500,000 miles from the sun. Express this distance in scientific notation.

         b. One gram is approximately 3.53×10^{-2} ounces. Express this number in decimal notation.

Solution: **a.** $92,500,000 = 9.25 \times 10^7$

         The decimal point must be moved 7 places to the left in the number 92,500,000 in order to get a number that is between 1 and 10.

         b. $3.53 \times 10^{-2} = 3.53 \times \dfrac{1}{10^2} = \dfrac{3.53}{100} = 0.0353$

Express each number using scientific notation.

14. 347,000,000

15. 0.0000716

16. 6000

17. 0.0000005

18. 7,600,000,000

19. 315×10^{-3}

20. 215.6×10^4

21. $51,000 \times 10^{-2}$

In Exercises 22–29, express each number in decimal notation.

22. 3.4×104

23. 6×10^{-3}

24. 9.23×10^{-6}

25. 5.4×10^7

26. 6.28×10^{10}

27. 0.0058×10^{-2}

28. 367.8×10^2

29. 348×10^{-4}

30. One ton is approximately 9.07×10^5 grams. About how many grams is 1000 tons?

31. One kilometer is approximately 3.94×10^4 inches. One kilometer is equal to 10^6 millimeters. About how many inches is equal to 1 millimeter?

Instructional Target: Analyze and/or solve problems involving quadratic situations

An equation that can be written in the form $ax^2 + bx + c = 0$ is a quadratic equation.
The solutions are given by the two parts of the quadratic formula shown below.

$$x = \frac{-b + \sqrt{b^2 - 4ac}}{2a}, \; x = \frac{-b - \sqrt{b^2 - 4ac}}{2a}$$

Example: A ball is hit into the air. The height reached by the ball in feet after t seconds is given by:

$$h(t) = -16t^2 + 46t.$$

After how many seconds will the ball be 33 feet above the ground?

Solution: Find the time when the value of h is 33.

$$33 = -16t^2 + 46t$$

Rewrite the equation in the form $ax^2 + bx + c = 0$ and solve using the quadratic formula. Add $16t^2$ and $-46t$ to both sides of the equation to get

$$16t^2 - 46t + 33 = 0.$$

Use the quadratic formula with $a = 16$, $b = -46$, and $c = 33$.

$$t = \frac{-(-46) \pm \sqrt{(-46)^2 - 4(16)(33)}}{2(16)}$$

$$= \frac{46 \pm \sqrt{4}}{32}$$

$$= \frac{46 \pm 2}{32}$$

$$t = \frac{48}{32} = 1.5 \text{ or } t = \frac{44}{32} = 1.375$$

The ball reaches a height of 33 feet at 1.375 seconds (on the way up) and it is at 33 feet again at 1.5 seconds (on the way back down).

Solve for x. Round answers to the nearest thousandth, if necessary.

32. $2x^2 + 3x = 5$ **33.** $x^2 = 5x + 6$ **34.** $3x^2 - x - 4 = 0$

35. $x^2 + 5x + 6 = 0$ **36.** $4x^2 - 2x = 3$ **37.** $6x - x^2 = -12$

38. $x^2 - x + 4 = 0$ **39.** $2x^2 - 2x = 7$ **40.** $3 + x = x^2$

41. $x^2 - x = 20$ **42.** $3x^2 + 2x = 4$ **43.** $5x^2 + x - 2 = 1$

Example: The income, in dollars, of a tour operator is given by $I(t) = 130t - 2t^2$, where t is the number of tickets sold. What is the tour operator's income if 10 tickets are sold?

Solution: Find the income when $t = 10$. Substitute $t = 10$ into the equation.

$$I(10) = 130(10) - 2(10)^2$$

$$= 1300 - 200$$

$$= 1100$$

The tour operator's income is $1100 when 10 tickets are sold.

PRACTICE WORKSHEETS

Solve each problem.

44. A square has sides of length $x^2 + 4$. Find the perimeter if $x = 4$.

45. A rectangle has a width of $2x^2 - 3x$ and a length of $x^2 + 5$. Find the area if $x = 3$.

46. A rectangle has a length of $2x + 4$ and a width of $3x - 1$.

    a. Write an equation for the area, A, of the rectangle.

    b. Find the area of the rectangle if $x = 4$.

47. A ball thrown from the roof of a building reaches a height in feet given by $h(t) = -16t^2 + 92t + 80$, where t is the time in seconds after it was thrown. Give the height reached by the ball after

    a. 2 seconds.   **b.** 4 seconds.   **c.** 6 seconds.

48. A baseball hit from home plate into the air reaches a height in feet given by $h(d) = -0.003d^2 + d + 3$, where d is the horizontal distance in feet between the ball and home plate. Give the height reached by the ball when its horizontal distance from home plate is

    a. 40 feet.   **b.** 100 feet.   **c.** 200 feet.

49. In Exercise 48, suppose that there is a fence that is 10 feet high at a distance of 360 feet from home plate. Will the ball go over the fence?

Instructional Target: Analyze and/or solve problems involving right triangles

The **Pythagorean theorem:** In a right triangle, the square of the length of the hypotenuse is equal to the sum of the squares of the lengths of the legs.

In the diagram, c is the length of the hypotenuse and a and b are the lengths of the legs, so $c^2 = a^2 + b^2$.

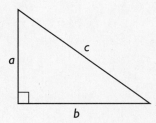

Example: A supporting wire is used to stabilize a telephone pole as shown. If the wire is to be attached to the pole at a distance of 16 feet from its base and to the ground at a distance of 12 feet from the base, what must be the length, x, of the wire?

Solution: Use the Pythagorean theorem. The legs have lengths 12 and 16 and the hypotenuse has length x.

$$x^2 = (12)^2 + (16)^2$$
$$= 144 + 256$$
$$= 400$$
$$x = \sqrt{400}, \text{ or } 20$$

The wire should be 20 feet long.

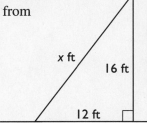

Find the value of *x* in each of the right triangles.

50.

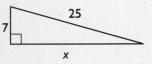

13

x

12

51.

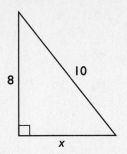

8   10

x

52.

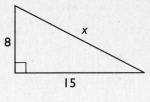

8   *x*

15

53.

25

7

x

54.

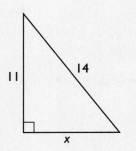

15

x

12

55.

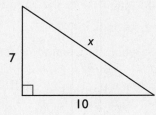

x

7

10

56.

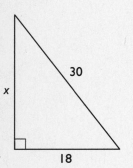

30

x

18

57.

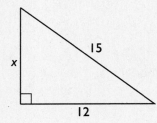

14

11

x

58.

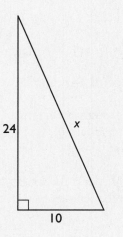

24   *x*

10

59.

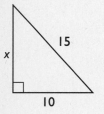

15

x

10

60.

x   41

9

61.

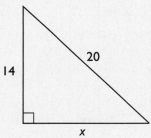

20

14

x

Preparing for the Texas Algebra I End-of-Course Exam
Copyright © McDougal Littell Inc. All rights reserved.

Cumulative Practice for Objective 8

1. There are 2 bacteria growing in a culture. Every hour the number of bacteria triples. After h hours there will be $B = 2 \cdot 3^h$ bacteria. How many bacteria will there be after 3 hours?

  A 9
  B 11
  C 18
  D 54
  E 216

2. One square mile is approximately 2.59×10^6 square meters. How many square meters is 100 square miles?

  A 2.59×10^3
  B 2.59×10^4
  C 2.59×10^8
  D 2.59×10^{12}
  E 2.59×10^{36}

3. A 1 pound ball bearing is dropped from the roof of the science building during an experiment. Its height above the ground, in feet, after t seconds is given by $h(t) = 80 - 16t^2$. What is the height of the ball bearing after 2 seconds?

  A 16 ft
  B 48 ft
  C 60 ft
  D 64 ft
  E 144 ft

4. Simplify $(a^2bc^0)^3$.

  A a^5b^3
  B $a^5b^4c^3$
  C a^6b^3c
  D a^6b^3
  E a^8b^3

5. The distance across a small pond is approximated by finding the distance between points A and B as shown in the diagram. What is the distance from point A to point B?

  A 10.6 m
  B 21.2 m
  C 40 m
  D 44 m
  E 56 m

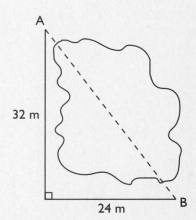

Practice for Objective 9

OBJECTIVE 9   The student will use problem-solving strategies to analyze, solve, and/or justify solutions to real-world and mathematical problems involving one-variable or two-variable situations.

Instructional Target: Analyze and/or solve problems involving one-variable situations

---

Example: Sarah has 7 more computer games than Sandra. Altogether, they have 27 computer games. How many computer games does Sarah have?

Solution: Let x be the number of computer games Sarah has. Since she has 7 more games than Sandra, Sandra has $x - 7$ games. Together, they have 27 games, so

$$x + (x - 7) = 27.$$

Solve the equation for x.

$x + (x - 7) = 27$	
$2x - 7 = 27$	Combine like terms.
$2x - 7 + 7 = 27 + 7$	Add 7 to both sides.
$2x = 34$	Simplify.
$x = 17$	Divide both sides by 2.

Sarah has 17 computer games.

Practice Exercises:

Solve.

1. Jimmy has $2.05 in nickels and dimes. He has 4 more dimes than nickels. How many nickels does Jimmy have?

2. The original price of a sweatshirt is x dollars. The sweatshirt is on sale for $\frac{1}{5}$ off the original price. If the sale price of the sweatshirt is $28, what is the original price of the sweatshirt?

3. A rectangle has a width of $x + 2$ feet and a length of $2x + 5$ feet. If the perimeter of the rectangle is 50 feet, find the width of the rectangle.

4. Linda and Doug earned $35 for painting their neighbor's fence. Doug is older and more experienced as a painter, so he earned $8 more than Linda. How much did Doug earn?

5. The cost of shipping a package overnight was $9.50. The company that shipped it charged $5 plus $.75 per pound. How much did the package weigh?

6. A rectangle is 7 inches longer than it is wide. If the perimeter is 42 inches, how long is the rectangle?

7. Arvid spent $7 buying apples and oranges. The apples cost $.50 per pound and the oranges cost $.75 per pound. If he bought twice as many pounds of apples as oranges, how many pounds of oranges did he buy?

8. Janaki earned $195 working in a retail store last week. She is paid a salary of $150 per week plus 3% of the total price of the merchandise she sells. What was the total price of the merchandise she sold last week?

9. Herman's Floor Refinishers charged $525 to refinish a wood floor. The rate they charge for refinishing a floor is $75 plus $3 per square foot of floor. What was the total area of the floor, in square feet, that they refinished.

10. The perimeter of a square is 8 more than 3 times the length of one side. What is the length of one side of the square?

11. Ingrid and Carlos have 57 marbles altogether. If Carlos has 13 more marbles than Ingrid, how many marbles does Carlos have?

12. Janet rented a bicycle for 5 hours one Saturday afternoon. The rental shop charged her a fee of $3.00 plus an hourly rate for the bicycle. If the total charge for the 5 hours was $25.50, what was the hourly rate that the rental shop charged?

13. Millie's car has depreciated in value since she purchased it several years ago. It is now worth $300 less than $\frac{1}{3}$ of its original price. If it is now worth $7300, how much was the original price?

14. Bert took three tests. He scored the same on the first two tests. On the third test, he scored 12 points higher than on each of the first two tests. If his average for all three tests was 82, what was his score on the first test?

15. A retail shoe store owner adds 20% to his cost to determine the retail selling price of his basketball shoes. If the retail selling price of a pair of basketball shoes was $114, what was the original cost of those shoes to the owner of the shoe store?

16. Angela has $3.20 in nickels, dimes, and quarters. She has 4 more nickels than quarters and she has 3 times as many dimes as quarters. How many quarters does she have?

Instructional Target: Analyze and/or solve problems involving two-variable situations

Example: Priscilla took her friends and all of their children to see a movie. Priscilla paid $58 altogether for the 11 people who went. If an adult ticket cost $7.50 and a child ticket cost $4.00, how many children went to the movie?

Solution: Let the number of adults be a and the number of children be c. There were 11 people who went to the movie, so

$$a + c = 11$$

Each adult ticket cost $7.50, so the total cost for the adults was $7.5a$. Each child ticket cost $4.00, so the total cost for all of the children was $4c$. The total cost for everyone was $58, so

$$7.5a + 4c = 58.$$

Solve the system of equations.

$$a + c = 11$$
$$7.5a + 4c = 58$$

Solve for a in the first equation, $a = 11 - c$, and use substitution in the second equation.

$7.5(11 - c) + 4c = 58$	Substitute $11 - c$ for a.
$82.5 - 7.5c + 4c = 58$	Use the distributive property.
$82.5 - 3.5c = 58$	Combine like terms.
$-3.5c = -24.5$	Subtract 82.5 from both sides.
$c = 7$	Divide both sides by -3.5.

There were 7 children who went to the movie.

For Exercises 17–22, write a system of equations that could be used to solve the problem. Then solve the problem.

17. The difference of two numbers is 12. The sum of the larger number and 3 times the smaller number is 20. Find the larger of the two numbers.

18. Jerry has 23 coins, all in nickels and dimes. If he has $1.95 altogether, find the number of nickels Jerry has.

19. Dolores bought 12 pizzas for a party she was giving for the Math Club. Some were pepperoni pizzas, which cost $11.00 each, and the rest were mushroom pizzas, which cost $9.50 each. Altogether, she paid $124.50 for the pizzas. How many pepperoni pizzas did she buy?

20. Three apples and 4 bananas sell for $1.60. One apple and 3 bananas sell for $.95. What is the cost of 1 banana?

21. The Manhattan Island Cruise Company sold 57 tickets for its Circle-the-Island Cruise. Each adult had to pay $22 for the cruise and each child had to pay $10. If the company's total receipts were $774, how many children went on the cruise?

22. Juanita invested $5000 in two different mutual funds. The growth fund earned 18% for the year and the social choice fund earned 14% for the year. Altogether, Juanita earned $780 for the year. How much did she invest in the growth fund?

Solve.

23. If $(x, 5)$ is a solution of the equation $6x - 3y = 21$, find the value of x.

24. The larger of two numbers is 7 more than twice the smaller of the two numbers. When the smaller number is added to 3 times the larger number the result is 42. Find the smaller of the two numbers.

25. If (a, b) is the point where the lines given by the equations $2x + 3y = 11$ and $x - 2y = -12$ intersect, find a.

26. Altogether, Min-Yang and Bill have 84 baseball cards. Bill has 3 times as many baseball cards as Min-Yang. How many baseball cards does Bill have?

27. Jamille wants to buy 16 pieces of candy so that she can give one to each of the other students in her Algebra I class. Red Hots cost 10 cents each and Jawbreakers cost 15 cents each. If Jamille spends all of the $2.10 she has to spend on the candy, how many Jawbreakers will she buy?

28. On Friday morning, Phyllis bought supplies for her niece's birthday party. She bought 8 hats and 3 piñatas for $36. Later that day, she found out that more children were coming to the party than she thought. She bought 4 more hats and one more piñata for $14. How much did she pay for each hat?

Cumulative Practice for Objective 9

1. The staff of a business office includes an office manager, a bookkeeper, a receptionist, and a supervisor for every 12 clerks. If there are 7 people on the staff, how many clerks are there?

   A 12
   B 19
   C 22
   D 48
   E 84

2. Mrs. Anderson bought 12 tickets to the local fair and spent $72. She bought child tickets for $4 each and she bought adult tickets for $7 each. How many adult tickets did she buy?

   A 10
   B 8
   C 6
   D 4
   E 2

3. A rectangle is 8 inches longer than it is wide. If the perimeter of the rectangle is 72 inches, what is the length of the rectangle?

   A 6 in.
   B 14 in.
   C 22 in.
   D 32 in.
   E 40 in.

4. Kareem and Jackie sold a total of $85 worth of raffle tickets. Kareem sold $15 more than Jackie. What was the total dollar value of the tickets that Jackie sold?

   A $20
   B $35
   C $50
   D $65
   E $0

5. There were 27 people in the school play. There were twice as many students in the play as teachers. How many students were in the play?

   A 6
   B 8
   C 12
   D 15
   E 18

PRACTICE WORKSHEETS

Practice for Objective 10

OBJECTIVE 10 The student will use problem-solving strategies to analyze, solve, and/or justify solutions to real-world and mathematical problems involving probability, ratio and proportion, or graphical and tabular data.

Instructional Target: Analyze and/or solve problems involving probability

The theoretical probability of an event is the ratio $\frac{\text{number of favorable outcomes}}{\text{total number of possible outcomes}}$, where an outcome is favorable if it makes the event happen.

Example: A standard six-sided die is rolled. What is the probability that the number rolled is less than 3?

Solution: There are 6 possible outcomes: 1, 2, 3, 4, 5, or 6. Two of these, 1 and 2, are favorable outcomes. The probability of rolling a number less than 3 is $\frac{2}{6}$, or $\frac{1}{3}$.

Practice Exercises:

Solve.

1. Ryan has 13 coins in his pocket. Five of them are pennies and the rest are nickels. If he pulls 1 coin out of his pocket at random, what is the probability that it will be a nickel?

2. A seven-sided die has 7 faces, which are numbered 1 through 7. If this die is rolled once, what is the probability that the number rolled will be odd?

3. Roberto has 15 marbles in a bag. Seven of the marbles are blue and the rest are red. If Roberto reaches into the bag and takes out 1 marble without looking, what is the probability that the marble will be red?

4. A card is selected at random from a standard deck of 52 playing cards. What is the probability that the card drawn is

   a. a queen?   **b.** a heart?

5. Albert has 17 beads in a hat. Twelve of the beads are black and the rest are white. Albert takes out 3 beads without looking. If all 3 of these beads are black, what is the probability that the next bead he takes from the hat (without looking) will be black?

6. Julius takes 2 cards at random from a standard deck of 52 playing cards. One is the ace of hearts and the other is the 10 of hearts. If Julius takes 1 card at random from the remaining 50 cards, what is the probability that it will be

   a. an ace?   **b.** a king?   **c.** a heart?   **d.** the 7 of clubs?

Sometimes probabilities are determined by performing an experiment. The experimental probability is the ratio $\dfrac{\text{the number of times the event occurs}}{\text{the total number of times the experiment is performed}}$.

Example: A basketball player has taken 85 free throws so far this season and she has made 68 of them. What is the probability that she will make her next free throw? How many free throws can she be expected to make out of the next 20 free throws she attempts?

Solution: The experimental probability of her making a free throw is

$$\dfrac{\text{the number of free throws made}}{\text{the total number of free throws attempted}} = \dfrac{68}{85} = \dfrac{4}{5}.$$

The probability that she will make her next free throw is $\dfrac{4}{5}$ or 0.8 or 80%. She can be expected to make $\dfrac{4}{5}$ of the number of free throws she attempts so she can be expected to make $\dfrac{4}{5}(20) = 16$ of the next 20 free throws she attempts.

Solve.

7. A baseball player pitched to 286 batters during the first 11 games he pitched. He struck out 47 of those batters. Using this information, what would you predict for the number of batters he will strike out of the next 24 batters he faces?

8. A light-bulb manufacturer randomly selects and tests its light bulbs for effectiveness. Of the first 957 bulbs that were tested, 11 were found to be defective. The bulbs are sold by the dozen. If James buys 1 dozen of the bulbs, how many can he expect to be defective? If Dieppa buys 8 dozen of the bulbs, how many can she expect to be defective?

9. Janice is searching for four-leafed clovers. So far she has found 98 clovers and 2 of them were four-leafed. If she searches until she has found 245 more clovers, how many four-leafed clovers can she expect to have altogether?

10. In the first 10 games of the football season, a quarterback threw 240 passes. He completed 144 of his passes, 12 of which were for touchdowns. If he throws an average of 20 passes per game for the next 6 games, how many passes can he expect to complete and how many of these passes can he expect to be for a touchdown?

PRACTICE WORKSHEETS

Instructional Target: Analyze and/or solve problems involving ratio and proportion

A **ratio** compares two numbers by division. Common forms for writing a ratio are

$$a \text{ to } b, \qquad a : b, \qquad \text{and} \qquad \frac{a}{b}.$$

When two ratios are set equal to each other as in $\frac{a}{b} = \frac{c}{d}$, the equation is called a **proportion**. Multiplying both sides of this equation by the common denominator, bd, gives the following *rule of proportions*.

$$ad = bc$$

Example: A 4 foot piece of pipe used in a sewer drain weighs 15 pounds. A certain job is being planned which will require 72 feet of the pipe. If a truck is used to transport the pipe from the warehouse to the job site, how much weight will the truck have to be able to carry?

Solution: The weight of the pipe is directly proportional to the length of the pipe. Set up a proportion and solve. Let x be the weight of the 72 feet of pipe.

$$\frac{\text{length of the piece of pipe}}{\text{weight of the piece of pipe}} = \frac{\text{total length of required pipe}}{\text{total weight of required pipe}}$$

$$\frac{4}{15} = \frac{72}{x}$$

$$\begin{array}{ll} (4)(x) = (15)(72) & \text{Rule of proportions} \\[2mm] x = \frac{(15)(72)}{4} & \text{Divide both sides by 4.} \\[2mm] x = 270 & \text{Simplify.} \end{array}$$

The truck will have to be able to carry 270 pounds of pipe.

Solve.

11. The Math Club bought 8 pizzas for a party at a total cost of $13. How much would they have had to pay for 12 pizzas?

12. A certain cookie recipe calls for 3 cups of flour and $\frac{1}{2}$ cup of sugar. Roger has 4 cups of flour and he decides to use all of it to make cookies. How much sugar does he need?

13. The ratio of girls to boys in Mr. Clark's Calculus I class is 4 to 3. If there are 15 boys in the class, how many students are in the class altogether?

14. The cost of shipping a package is directly proportional to the weight of the package. If it costs $8.50 to ship a package weighing 3 pounds, how much will it cost to ship a package weighing 7.5 pounds?

15. The ratio of the number of teeth on two connecting gears is 4 to 3. If the larger gear has 92 teeth, how many teeth does the smaller gear have?

16. The amount of simple interest earned on a savings account in one year is directly proportional to the amount of money in the account. If $50 in simple interest is earned on an account containing $1250, how much interest would be earned on an account containing $1900?

17. The scale for a certain map is 12 centimeters to 80 kilometers. If a lake drawn on the map has a length of 2 cm, what is the actual length of the lake?

18. Human hair grows approximately 50 millimeters every 2 months. How many millimeters will your hair grow in 1 year?

19. In mixing a fruit punch for a party, Geoffrey is using orange juice, pineapple juice, and cranberry juice in a ratio of 5:2:1. If he already has 8 quarts of orange juice and 2 quarts of pineapple juice in the punch bowl,

    a. how much pineapple juice does he need to add to the bowl?

    b. how much cranberry juice does he need to add to the bowl?

20. Two pieces of string are needed for the construction of a science-project model. The lengths of the pieces of string to be used must be in a ratio of 3 to 2. If the shorter piece required has a length of 26 inches, how long must the longer piece of string be?

21. Peggy owned 17 compact discs and Dot owned 12 compact discs. After they both purchased some new compact discs, the ratio of the number of Peggy's compact discs to Dot's compact discs was 5 to 4. If Peggy purchased 3 new compact discs, how many new compact discs did Dot purchase?

22. Janaki has 17 marbles in a bag. Ten of the marbles are red and the rest are blue. If she adds 8 red marbles to the bag, how many blue marbles will she have to add if she wants the final ratio of red marbles to blue marbles to be 3 to 2?

23. A piece of wood that is 7 feet long is to be cut into two pieces so that the ratio of the lengths of the two pieces is 9 to 5. How long should each piece be?

24. Ralph rode his bicycle 4.5 miles in 0.75 hour. At this rate, how long would it take him to ride his bicycle an additional 6 miles?

25. The amount of sales tax paid to purchase an item is directly proportional to the price of the item. If the sales tax on an item priced at $4.50 is $.20, what would be the sales tax on an item priced at $8.10?

Instructional Target: Analyze graphical and tabular data including scatter plots and/or make predictions based on the data

Example: It is January, mathematics project time at Phillip's grade school, and Phillip is doing a study of the students attending his school. So far, he has found the average height for students in the first, second, fourth, and fifth grades, and he has plotted the results as shown at the right. According to the graph, what is the best estimate for the average height of the students in third grade?

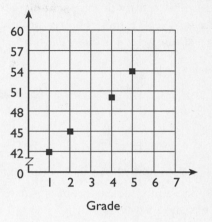

Solution: The points that have been plotted appear to fall nearly along a line. Plotting a point for Grade 3 (the star) so that all of the points appear to be on the same line shows the average height of the students in third grade to be about 48 inches.

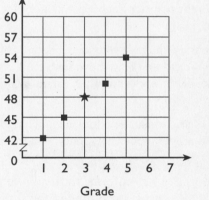

Answer each question.

26. Using the information given in the example above, what do you expect the average height of the students in sixth grade to be?

27. Using the information given in the example above, in which grade do you expect to find a student whose height is

a. 45.5 inches?   **b.** 55 inches?

28. Using the information given in the example above, what do you expect the average height of the students in seventh grade to be?

29. Use the information given in the example above. It is now July, six months after the project was done, and Phillip is 53.25 inches tall. Which grade will Phillip most likely be entering when school begins again in September?

PRACTICE WORKSHEETS

During one year, Jeremy kept track of the money his family spent on gas and tolls and the total distance traveled for each of the trips taken by him and his family during school vacations and over the summer. The results he obtained are summarized in the graph at the right.

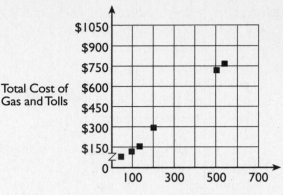

Use the graph at the right above to answer Exercises 30–33.

30. Jeremy and his family took a trip of approximately 200 miles. About how much did it cost for gas and tolls for this trip?

31. If Jeremy and his family were to take a trip where the total distance covered was about 400 miles, about how much could they expect to have to spend in gas and tolls for the trip?

32. Jeremy's parents have saved some money for a family vacation. Now they must choose a place to go. They have budgeted $2500 for food and lodging and $850 for transportation (gas and tolls). About how far away from their home can the vacation spot be?

33. If Jeremy's family takes two trips next summer, one of 300 miles and the other covering 500 miles, about how much will they have to spend on gas and tolls?

34. The table at the right shows the amount Central High School paid for uniforms for its junior varsity boys' basketball team. According to the table, what is the best estimate of the amount that will have to be spent on uniforms in 1999?

35. According to the table given in Exercise 34, what is the best estimate of the amount that Central High would have had to spend on uniforms if the school had purchased uniforms in 1989?

Year	Cost
1984	$230
1987	$320
1990	$410
1993	$500
1996	$590

36. The table to the right shows the resale value for Hannah's car. According to the table, how much will Hannah's car be worth in 1999?

37. According to the table in Exercise 36, in what year will Hannah's car begin to have no resale value?

Year	Resale Value
1993	$8600
1994	$7050
1995	$5650
1996	$4400
1997	$3300

Preparing for the Texas Algebra I End-of-Course Exam

Cumulative Practice for Objective 10

1. Caroline made cookies and put them into a jar. There were 6 raisin cookies and 1 dozen chocolate chip cookies in the jar. Her brother Seth took out 2 raisin cookies. If Caroline now takes out 1 cookie without looking, what is the probability that it will be a raisin cookie?

   A $\frac{2}{9}$

   B $\frac{1}{4}$

   C $\frac{1}{3}$

   D $\frac{2}{3}$

   E $\frac{3}{4}$

2. Ali has thrown 63 darts at a target and hit the center circle 9 times. Which is the best estimate of the number of times he will hit the center circle if he throws 48 more darts?

   A 13
   B 10
   C 7
   D 4
   E 1

3. A certain recipe calls for the use of flour, sugar, and oatmeal in the ratio of 2:3:1. If 5 cups of flour are used, how many cups of sugar should be used?

   A 1.2
   B 2.5
   C 3.3
   D 6
   E 7.5

4. The number of tadpoles produced at a frog farm is directly proportional to the number of adult frogs at the farm. If 120 adult frogs produce 4200 tadpoles, how many tadpoles would be produced by 150 adult frogs?

   A 3150
   B 3360
   C 4230
   D 5250
   E 5600

5. Jasmine has been having her stamp and coin collection appraised each year. The value of the collection is given in the table. According to the table, how much will Jasmine's collection be worth in 1998?

   A $3275
   B $3450
   C $3800
   D $3975
   E $4150

Year	Cost
1993	$1100
1994	$1325
1995	$1725
1996	$2300
1997	$3050

PRACTICE WORKSHEETS

FORMULA CHART
ALGEBRA I END-OF-COURSE EXAMINATION

Perimeter	square	$P = 4s$
	rectangle	$P = 2(l + w)$
Circumference	circle	$C = 2\pi r$
Area	square	$A = s^2$
	rectangle	$A = lw$ or $A = bh$
	triangle	$A = \dfrac{bh}{2}$
	trapezoid	$A = \dfrac{1}{2}(b_1 + b_2)h$
	circle	$A = \pi r^2$
Surface Area	cube	$S = 6s^2$
	cylinder (lateral)	$S = 2\pi rh$
Volume	rectangular prism	$V = lwh$
	cylinder	$V = \pi r^2 h$
	cube	$V = s^3$
Pythagorean Theorem	right triangle	$a^2 + b^2 = c^2$

Distance Formula	$d = \sqrt{(x_1 - x_2)^2 + (y_1 - y_2)^2}$
Slope of a Line	$m = \dfrac{y_2 - y_1}{x_2 - x_1}$
Quadratic Formula	$x = \dfrac{-b \pm \sqrt{b^2 - 4ac}}{2a}$
Slope-Intercept Form of an Equation	$y = mx + b$
Point-Slope Form of an Equation	$y - y_1 = m(x - x_1)$
Standard Form of an Equation	$Ax + By = C$

ADDITIONAL RESOURCES

Using the EOC Practice Exams to Guide Your Skills Review

This *Preparing for the Algebra I End-of-Course Exam* booklet includes two practice exams. You can use your results on these exams to guide your review of the math skills needed to master the Algebra I End-of-Course (EOC) objectives. (For a listing of the EOC objectives, see the correlation on pages viii–x.)

Practice Exam 1 is a *diagnostic* exam. Responses to Practice Exam 1 should be entered on version 1 of the EOC Practice Exam Answer Sheet included with this booklet. Compare your responses to the correct answers given in the Teacher's Edition of this booklet. A completed answer sheet is shown and explained below. Use this answer sheet to analyze your results.

Each row of answers corresponds to questions for a specific EOC objective. For example, questions 2, 12, 22, and 32 all correspond to EOC Objective 2: Graphing

EOC Practice Exam Answer Sheet (version 1)

NAME Maria Diaz   DATE 9/23/97   NUMBER CORRECT 36

Solve each problem. For all questions except 4, 14, 24, and 34 decide which answer is the best of the choices given and then fill in the corresponding oval next to question number. For Questions 4, 14, 24, and 34, write your answer in the boxes next to the question number and then fill in the corresponding ovals below the boxes. Note that Questions 41–48 are optional; your teacher will tell you whether you should answer those questions.

3/4 1. Characteristics of graphing
3/4 2. Graphing
2/4 3. Equations of lines
4/4 4. Linear eqns./ineqs./systems

On the blank line next to each EOC objective, you can enter the number correct out of the number possible. Objective 9 has 8 questions; all the others have 4. Objective 5 has an additional 4 questions that are optional.

4/4 5. Quadratic equations
1/4 6. Polynomials
3/4 8. Exp./quad./rt.triangles
7/4 9. One/two variables
3/4 10. Prob./ratio & prop./data

Optional Questions

4/4 5. Absolute value eqns./ineqs.
2/4 7. Rational/radical equations

If you have one or more incorrect answers for a particular objective, you may want to complete the practice worksheet for that objective (see pages 57–111).

If a response is incorrect, be sure to review that question. Try to determine the cause of your error.

For Practice Exam 2, the sequence of questions has been randomized to create an exam that is similar to actual EOC exams. Because of this, you cannot use version 1 of the EOC Practice Exam Answer Sheet; use version 2 instead. The answers to this exam are also in the Teacher's Edition of this booklet, which also includes a correlation of the exam questions to the EOC objectives. By using this correlation, you can use this exam diagnostically as well.

You can use the summary sheet on page 121 to record your test scores, and to keep track of your progress as you complete each practice worksheet in this booklet.

ADDITIONAL RESOURCES

115

EOC Practice Exam Answer Sheet (version 1)

NAME ______________________ DATE ______________ NUMBER CORRECT ____________

Solve each problem. For all questions except 4, 14, 24, and 34 decide which answer is the best of the choices given and then fill in the corresponding oval next to question number. For Questions 4, 14, 24, and 34, write your answer in the boxes next to the question number and then fill in the corresponding ovals below the boxes. Note that Questions 41–48 are optional; your teacher will tell you whether you should answer those questions.

1 Ⓐ Ⓑ Ⓒ Ⓓ Ⓔ	11 Ⓕ Ⓖ Ⓗ Ⓙ Ⓚ	21 Ⓐ Ⓑ Ⓒ Ⓓ Ⓔ	31 Ⓐ Ⓑ Ⓒ Ⓓ Ⓔ	____ 1 Characteristics of graphing
2 Ⓕ Ⓖ Ⓗ Ⓙ Ⓚ	12 Ⓐ Ⓑ Ⓒ Ⓓ Ⓔ	22 Ⓕ Ⓖ Ⓗ Ⓙ Ⓚ	32 Ⓕ Ⓖ Ⓗ Ⓙ Ⓚ	____ 2 Graphing
3 Ⓐ Ⓑ Ⓒ Ⓓ Ⓔ	13 Ⓕ Ⓖ Ⓗ Ⓙ Ⓚ	23 Ⓐ Ⓑ Ⓒ Ⓓ Ⓔ	33 Ⓐ Ⓑ Ⓒ Ⓓ Ⓔ	____ 3 Equations of lines
4 [ ][ ][ ][ ] . [ ] + − 0 1 2 3 4 5 6 7 8 9	14 [ ][ ][ ][ ] . [ ] + − 0 1 2 3 4 5 6 7 8 9	24 [ ][ ][ ][ ] . [ ] + − 0 1 2 3 4 5 6 7 8 9	34 [ ][ ][ ][ ] . [ ] + − 0 1 2 3 4 5 6 7 8 9	____ 4 Linear eqns./ineqs./systems
5 Ⓕ Ⓖ Ⓗ Ⓙ Ⓚ	15 Ⓐ Ⓑ Ⓒ Ⓓ Ⓔ	25 Ⓐ Ⓑ Ⓒ Ⓓ Ⓔ	35 Ⓕ Ⓖ Ⓗ Ⓙ Ⓚ	____ 5 Quadratic equations
6 Ⓐ Ⓑ Ⓒ Ⓓ Ⓔ	16 Ⓕ Ⓖ Ⓗ Ⓙ Ⓚ	26 Ⓕ Ⓖ Ⓗ Ⓙ Ⓚ	36 Ⓐ Ⓑ Ⓒ Ⓓ Ⓔ	____ 6 Polynomials
7 Ⓕ Ⓖ Ⓗ Ⓙ Ⓚ	17 Ⓐ Ⓑ Ⓒ Ⓓ Ⓔ	27 Ⓐ Ⓑ Ⓒ Ⓓ Ⓔ	37 Ⓕ Ⓖ Ⓗ Ⓙ Ⓚ	____ 8 Exp./quad./rt. triangles
8 Ⓐ Ⓑ Ⓒ Ⓓ Ⓔ	18 Ⓕ Ⓖ Ⓗ Ⓙ Ⓚ	28 Ⓕ Ⓖ Ⓗ Ⓙ Ⓚ	38 Ⓐ Ⓑ Ⓒ Ⓓ Ⓔ	____ 9 One/two variables
9 Ⓕ Ⓖ Ⓗ Ⓙ Ⓚ	19 Ⓐ Ⓑ Ⓒ Ⓓ Ⓔ	29 Ⓐ Ⓑ Ⓒ Ⓓ Ⓔ	39 Ⓕ Ⓖ Ⓗ Ⓙ Ⓚ	
10 Ⓐ Ⓑ Ⓒ Ⓓ Ⓔ	20 Ⓕ Ⓖ Ⓗ Ⓙ Ⓚ	30 Ⓕ Ⓖ Ⓗ Ⓙ Ⓚ	40 Ⓐ Ⓑ Ⓒ Ⓓ Ⓔ	____ 10 Prob./ratio & prop./data

Optional Questions

41 Ⓕ Ⓖ Ⓗ Ⓙ Ⓚ	43 Ⓕ Ⓖ Ⓗ Ⓙ Ⓚ	45 Ⓕ Ⓖ Ⓗ Ⓙ Ⓚ	47 Ⓕ Ⓖ Ⓗ Ⓙ Ⓚ	____ 5 Absolute value eqns./ineqs.
42 Ⓐ Ⓑ Ⓒ Ⓓ Ⓔ	44 Ⓐ Ⓑ Ⓒ Ⓓ Ⓔ	46 Ⓐ Ⓑ Ⓒ Ⓓ Ⓔ	48 Ⓐ Ⓑ Ⓒ Ⓓ Ⓔ	____ 7 Rational/radical equations

EOC Practice Exam Answer Sheet (version 2)

NAME _____ DATE _____ NUMBER CORRECT _____

Solve each problem. For Questions 1–3, write your answer in the boxes next to the question number and then fill in the corresponding ovals below the boxes. For Questions 4–40, decide which answer is the best of the choices given and then fill in the corresponding oval next to the question number. Note that Questions 41–48 are optional; your teacher will tell you whether you should answer those questions.

1

+	⓪	⓪	⓪		⓪
−	①	①	①		①
	②	②	②		②
	③	③	③		③
	④	④	④		④
	⑤	⑤	⑤		⑤
	⑥	⑥	⑥		⑥
	⑦	⑦	⑦		⑦
	⑧	⑧	⑧		⑧
	⑨	⑨	⑨		⑨

2

+	⓪	⓪	⓪		⓪
−	①	①	①		①
	②	②	②		②
	③	③	③		③
	④	④	④		④
	⑤	⑤	⑤		⑤
	⑥	⑥	⑥		⑥
	⑦	⑦	⑦		⑦
	⑧	⑧	⑧		⑧
	⑨	⑨	⑨		⑨

3

+	⓪	⓪	⓪		⓪
−	①	①	①		①
	②	②	②		②
	③	③	③		③
	④	④	④		④
	⑤	⑤	⑤		⑤
	⑥	⑥	⑥		⑥
	⑦	⑦	⑦		⑦
	⑧	⑧	⑧		⑧
	⑨	⑨	⑨		⑨

4 Ⓐ Ⓑ Ⓒ Ⓓ Ⓔ   23 Ⓕ Ⓖ Ⓗ Ⓙ Ⓚ
5 Ⓕ Ⓖ Ⓗ Ⓙ Ⓚ   24 Ⓐ Ⓑ Ⓒ Ⓓ Ⓔ
6 Ⓐ Ⓑ Ⓒ Ⓓ Ⓔ   25 Ⓕ Ⓖ Ⓗ Ⓙ Ⓚ
7 Ⓕ Ⓖ Ⓗ Ⓙ Ⓚ   26 Ⓐ Ⓑ Ⓒ Ⓓ Ⓔ
8 Ⓐ Ⓑ Ⓒ Ⓓ Ⓔ   27 Ⓕ Ⓖ Ⓗ Ⓙ Ⓚ
9 Ⓕ Ⓖ Ⓗ Ⓙ Ⓚ   28 Ⓐ Ⓑ Ⓒ Ⓓ Ⓔ
10 Ⓐ Ⓑ Ⓒ Ⓓ Ⓔ   29 Ⓕ Ⓖ Ⓗ Ⓙ Ⓚ
11 Ⓕ Ⓖ Ⓗ Ⓙ Ⓚ   30 Ⓐ Ⓑ Ⓒ Ⓓ Ⓔ
12 Ⓐ Ⓑ Ⓒ Ⓓ Ⓔ   31 Ⓕ Ⓖ Ⓗ Ⓙ Ⓚ
13 Ⓕ Ⓖ Ⓗ Ⓙ Ⓚ   32 Ⓐ Ⓑ Ⓒ Ⓓ Ⓔ
14 Ⓐ Ⓑ Ⓒ Ⓓ Ⓔ   33 Ⓕ Ⓖ Ⓗ Ⓙ Ⓚ
15 Ⓕ Ⓖ Ⓗ Ⓙ Ⓚ   34 Ⓐ Ⓑ Ⓒ Ⓓ Ⓔ
16 Ⓐ Ⓑ Ⓒ Ⓓ Ⓔ   35 Ⓕ Ⓖ Ⓗ Ⓙ Ⓚ
17 Ⓕ Ⓖ Ⓗ Ⓙ Ⓚ   36 Ⓐ Ⓑ Ⓒ Ⓓ Ⓔ
18 Ⓐ Ⓑ Ⓒ Ⓓ Ⓔ   37 Ⓕ Ⓖ Ⓗ Ⓙ Ⓚ
19 Ⓕ Ⓖ Ⓗ Ⓙ Ⓚ   38 Ⓐ Ⓑ Ⓒ Ⓓ Ⓔ
20 Ⓐ Ⓑ Ⓒ Ⓓ Ⓔ   39 Ⓕ Ⓖ Ⓗ Ⓙ Ⓚ
21 Ⓕ Ⓖ Ⓗ Ⓙ Ⓚ   40 Ⓐ Ⓑ Ⓒ Ⓓ Ⓔ
22 Ⓐ Ⓑ Ⓒ Ⓓ Ⓔ

Optional Questions

41 Ⓕ Ⓖ Ⓗ Ⓙ Ⓚ   45 Ⓕ Ⓖ Ⓗ Ⓙ Ⓚ
42 Ⓐ Ⓑ Ⓒ Ⓓ Ⓔ   46 Ⓐ Ⓑ Ⓒ Ⓓ Ⓔ
43 Ⓕ Ⓖ Ⓗ Ⓙ Ⓚ   47 Ⓕ Ⓖ Ⓗ Ⓙ Ⓚ
44 Ⓐ Ⓑ Ⓒ Ⓓ Ⓔ   48 Ⓐ Ⓑ Ⓒ Ⓓ Ⓔ

ADDITIONAL RESOURCES

Summary Sheet

Use this summary sheet to track your progress toward mastering the EOC objectives. Record the date on which you take each practice exam. After you have scored a *diagnostic* practice exam, (Practice Exam 1), enter the number correct for each objective (from version 1 of the answer sheets) in the appropriate box. After you have scored Practice Exam 2, use the "Item" column, which lists the question numbers corresponding to each objective, to correlate your responses (from version 2 of the answer sheets) to each EOC objective. Then enter the number correct for each objective in the "Score" column. If a score indicates the need to complete the practice worksheet that reviews an EOC objective, check the appropriate "Practice Worksheet" box, and later record the date on which you completed the worksheet.

EOC Objective	Practice Exam 1 Score	Practice Exam 2 Item	Practice Exam 2 Score	Practice Worksheet
Date of Exam:				
1: Characteristics of graphing	— / 4	31 32 33 38	— / 4	
2: Graphing	— / 4	29 30 35 39	— / 4	
3: Equations of lines	— / 4	34 36 37 40	— / 4	
4: Linear equations/inequalities/systems	— / 4	03 05 06 12	— / 4	
5: Quadratic equations	— / 4	07 08 13 14	— / 4	
6: Polynomials	— / 4	04 09 10 11	— / 4	
8: Exponents/quadratics/right triangles	— / 4	17 18 20 26	— / 4	
9: One- and two-variable situations	— / 8	01 02 15 16 19 21 25 28	— / 8	
10: Probability/ratio and proportion/data	— / 4	22 23 24 27	— / 4	
Total Score	**— / 40**		**— / 40**	
Optional Questions				
5: Absolute value equations/inequalities	— / 4	43 44 47 48	— / 4	
7: Rational/radical equations	— / 4	41 42 45 46	— / 4	

ADDITIONAL RESOURCES